WEBER'S ON THE GRILL: **STEAK & SIDES**

Table of Contents

4 INTRODUCTION

6 GRILLING FUNDAMENTALS

14 STEAK RECIPES

110 SIDES

126 RUBS

129 MARINADES

132 SAUCES

134 GRILLING GUIDE FOR STEAKS

136 GRILLING GUIDE FOR VEGGIES

138 SAFETY

140 INDEX

Anthropologists explain that hundreds of thousands of years ago civilization began when our ancestors first cooked meat over fire. Before then, we were nomads roaming from place to place and surviving mostly on raw food. When we sat down around a fire and cooked meat together night after night, all sorts of civilized things developed—like art, language, agriculture, and long-standing communities.

I can only imagine how tough and gamy the meat was way back then (think wild, muscular yaks), especially compared to the luscious beef steaks offered in stores today. Clearly we've made some progress in the quality of meat and, under the right conditions, it is now amazingly easy to grill great steaks.

This book is largely about improving those conditions. In other words, it provides you with all the latest grilling techniques you will need and it also lays out a wide array of fresh ideas for the best cuts of steak.

I know that many grillers put their highest priority on the steak itself. They don't want a lot of other ingredients and flavors cluttering the plate. Maybe just some spices or herbs, but that's it. For those of you in this camp, I have included some straight-up recipes like Top Sirloin Steak with Sante Fe Spice Rub (page 84) and Porterhouse Steaks with Herbed Vinaigrette (page 62). These are pure, simple, and absolutely delicious. For those grillers who like a little more pizzazz with their steaks, and perhaps something a little unexpected in the mix of flavors, I've got some really nice options, for example, Rib-Eye Steaks with Chipotle Butter (page 26) and New York Steaks with Toasted Fennel Spice Rub (page 32).

STEAK & SIDES

by Jamie Purviance

Photography by Tim Turner

Author	Jamie Purviance
Managing editor	Marsha Capen
Photographer and photo art direction	Tim Turner
Food stylist	Lynn Gagné
Assistant food stylist	Nina Albazi
Photo assistant	Christy Clow
Digital guru	Takamasa Ota
Indexer	Becky LaBrum
Color imaging and in-house prepress	Weber Creative Services
Contributors	Jessica Bard, Elizabeth Brown, Carolynn Carreño, Katherine Cobbs, April Cooper, Sarah Epstein, Lillian Kang, Kevin Kolman, Janet McCracken, Louisa Neumann, Tripp Rion, Rick Rodgers, Anne Martin Rolke, Cheryl Sternman Rule, Bob and Coleen Simmons, James Temple
Design and production	rabble+rouser, inc. Christina Schroeder, Chief Rouser Marsha Capen, Editorial Director Shum Prats, Creative Director Elaine Chow, Art Director Erick Collier, Interactive Art Director
Weber-Stephen Products Co.	Mike Kempster Sr., Executive Vice President Sherry L. Bale, Director, Public Relations Brooke Jones, Marketing Manager
Round Mountain Media	Susan Maruyama, Consulting Publishing Director
Oxmoor House, Inc.	Jim Childs, Vice President and Publishing Director Fonda Hitchcock, Brand Manager Susan Payne Dobbs, Editorial Director

10 9 8 7 6 5 4 3 2 1

ISBN-10: 0-376-02033-4
ISBN-13: 978-0-376-02033-8
Library of Congress Control Number: 2009941653

Weber Customer Service: 1.800.446.1071

www.weber.com® • www.sunset.com • www.oxmoorhouse.com • www.rabbleandrouser.com

Things can get even more interesting when you bring marinades, glazes, and sauces to the party, because now you can layer a series of flavors, one on top of the other. Along those lines I've given you some steak house classics, such as Porterhouse Steaks with Béarnaise Sauce (page 64) and Rib-Eye Steaks with Red Wine Sauce (page 21). Fortunately you can make these recipes at home with ingredients sold in almost any well-stocked supermarket. The prep time needed for these (and most of the recipes in this book) is under thirty minutes. Add a stellar side dish or two from the back of this book, and you're living a carnivore's dream.

With some other recipes I let my imagination run a little wild and developed some newly minted ideas that I hope will inspire you to try some tastes and techniques you may not know yet. I recommend Miso-Marinated Flatiron Steaks with Shiitake Mushrooms (page 104), Filet Mignon Steaks with Crab Guacamole (page 44), and Tagliata of Flank Steak with Arugula and Shaved Parmesan (page 68).

There's nothing highfalutin or intimidating about any of the recipes in this book. You won't need any high-tech kitchen tools or complicated tricks. These are no-nonsense recipes for casual nights when you just feel like a great steak. Invite some friends and family to join you, pour some drinks, and step outside. When the steaks hit the hot grate and you smell the smoke from searing meat, it is bound to light up your anticipation. After hundreds of thousands of years, the powerful effects of meat and fire have worked their way into our DNA. For us, a perfectly civilized way to end the day begins around the grill with steaks and sides.

Jamie Purviance

Grilling Fundamentals

WHAT TO LOOK FOR IN STEAK

Buy with an eye for flavor.

MARBLING

Beef should have a coarse marbling of milky white fat running through it. If the marbling is minimal or if the fat has a brown or yellow tint (a sign of old, dry meat), avoid it. Also avoid meat with large clumps of fat within the flesh. The thin marbling will melt and give the flesh richness and juiciness; the large clumps can be greasy and cause flare-ups.

COLOR

The flesh should have a rich pink or light cherry appearance. If it has a deep red or other dark color, there's a good chance it came from a dairy cow and the meat will be bland and tough.

MOISTURE

The surface should be moist, but not wet or sticky. A cut of meat that has been individually wrapped should not have much liquid in the package. That would indicate that the meat had been frozen and thawed.

DO GRADES MATTER?

Well, yes. Meat producers pay the United States Department of Agriculture (USDA) to grade their beef if they believe the quality is high enough. Only about two percent of beef gets the very top grade, "prime," and most of that is sold to restaurants. The second highest grade is "choice," which reflects generous marbling and tender meat. If you see a grade of "select" or no grade at all, maybe you should grill chicken that day. The beef is likely to be dry and chewy.

WHAT YOU NEED TO KNOW

Once you have selected just the right steak, there are seven simple steps for pulling a perfect steak off the grill every time. Follow them and you (and your steaks) will be the talk of the town.

GIVE IT A REST. Prior to grilling, remove your steak from the refrigerator and allow it to stand at room temperature for 15 to 30 minutes. Why? First, the fibers in the meat relax, producing more tenderness after cooking. Second, a properly rested steak will cook faster than a cold one, which means less moisture will be lost.

TRIM IT DOWN. You will want to leave a small layer of fat around the edges of your steak to add flavor, but don't overdo it. Trim all but ¼ inch of fat around the outer edge. Any more than that could lead to flare-ups.

OIL IT UP. That's right. It doesn't seem necessary to oil a steak with lots of marbling, but it helps prevent sticking. No need to slather it on; a very light coating of extra-virgin olive oil will do. Avoid oiling the cooking grates. Oil on a hot cooking grate by itself burns very quickly, creating unpleasant bitter flavors.

SPRINKLE ON THE SALT. If you are grilling a steak and not using a recipe, salt the steak 15 to 30 minutes before it goes on the grill. The salt will begin to mingle with the juices, which helps to develop a delicious crust on the steak when it is on the grill. But salting a steak too far ahead of time can be risky because the salt crystals have a tendency to draw moisture out of the meat over hours and hours. Kosher salt with its larger crystals and pure flavor is the salt of choice because it is less likely to dissolve completely and lose its character.

KEEP AN EYE ON THINGS. Unless it is a very thick cut, most steaks require less than 10 minutes total cooking time on the grill, so refrain from multi-tasking when the steak is on. Usually you'll want to start by searing the steak over direct high heat. Make sure the grill is good and hot and the cooking grates are nice and clean before placing the steak on the grill. This is critical for a good sear. After you've seared the steak, continue cooking over direct or indirect heat, depending on the thickness of the steak. (Consult the grilling guide on page 134 for suggested cooking times.) While you are grilling, remember to keep the lid down. It will keep the heat up and speed up the cooking time.

FORGO THE FORK. Meat forks are intended to help lift large roasts from the grill, not for flipping steaks or poking your meat while it cooks. Doing so will cause precious juices to escape, which will dry out your steak. Turn your steak with a pair of tongs instead.

GIVE IT A REST … AGAIN. After you remove your steak from the grill, allow it to rest for 3 to 5 minutes. This allows the juices that were pushed to the center of the meat by the heat of the grill to migrate back to all parts of the steak so you have juiciness throughout.

KNOW YOUR CUTS OF STEAK

The following cuts are particularly well suited for the grill—tender, juicy, and flavorful.

PORTERHOUSE

This is the classic steak house steak that features both a strip steak and filet mignon, separated by a bone.

T-BONE

A T-bone is just like a porterhouse except the piece of filet mignon is not as big, because this steak is cut a little farther forward on the animal.

STRIP

A New York strip is a relatively lean cut with a firmer texture than a rib-eye or filet mignon, but the flavor is great.

FILET MIGNON

Pricey and velvety soft, filets mignons make a nice splurge for special guests, though it's really the tenderness you are buying.

BONE-IN RIB-EYE

This incredibly tender and succulent steak includes an actual rib, which adds even more flavor.

RIB-EYE

A rib-eye steak's abundant internal fat melting into the meat creates one of the juiciest steak-eating experiences imaginable.

FLANK

You can quickly spot this steak by its flat oval shape and its long, clearly defined grain. Minimize the chewy effect of the grain by slicing across it.

FLATIRON

The flatiron is nestled into a tender area of the shoulder, so it's an exception to the rule that shoulder steaks are always tough. Plus it's cheap.

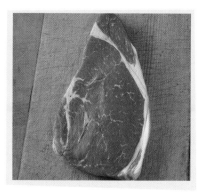

TOP SIRLOIN

This flat, firmly grained steak brings kabobs quickly to mind because it's so easy to cut it into solid cubes.

HANGER

Each animal has only one hanger steak, weighing in at about 2 pounds. The beefy flavor is enormous, but a tendon runs down the center of each one, so cut that out before grilling.

SKIRT

Like the flank steak, the coarsely grained skirt steak is cut from the chest area of the animal, so "chewiness" is an issue, but the taste is fabulous.

TRI-TIP

A tri-tip is taken from the sirloin area. It's not so much a steak as it is a skinny roast, but you can grill it like a thick steak. Just don't overcook it.

Grilling Fundamentals

GRILLING KNOW-HOW

THE DIFFERENCE BETWEEN DIRECT AND INDIRECT COOKING

With direct heat, the fire is right below the food. With indirect heat, the fire is off to one side of the grill, or on both sides of the grill, and the food sits over the unlit part.

Direct heat works great for small, tender pieces of food that cook quickly, such as steaks, hamburgers, chops, boneless chicken pieces, fish fillets, shellfish, and sliced vegetables. It sears the surfaces of these foods, developing flavors, texture, and delicious caramelization. If you leave steaks over direct heat long enough, it will cook them all the way to the center.

Indirect heat is generally better for larger, tougher foods that require longer cooking times, such as beef roasts, whole chickens, and ribs, but it is also a smart way to finish thick steaks that have been seared or browned first over direct heat, because you are less likely to burn them with indirect heat.

SETTING UP YOUR CHARCOAL GRILL FOR DIRECT AND INDIRECT COOKING

First things first. You'll need fuel, and the simplest way to measure the right amount of fuel for your charcoal grill is to use a chimney starter. Use it like a measuring cup for charcoal. Fill it to the rim with briquettes or lump charcoal, and burn them until they are lightly covered with ash.

Spread the coals in a tightly packed, single layer across one-half to two-thirds of the charcoal grate. Put the cooking grate in place, close the lid, and let the coals burn down to the desired heat. Leave all the vents open. This basic configuration is called a two-zone fire because you have one zone of direct heat and one zone of indirect heat. It's the setup you'll use most often. The temperature of a two-zone fire can be high, medium, or low, depending on how much charcoal is burning and how long it has been burning. Remember, charcoal loses heat over time.

few minutes and then reconnect the hose. Try lighting the grill again. If you still smell gas, shut the grill down and call Weber Customer Service.

You can switch from direct to indirect heat almost immediately. Just turn off one or more of the burners and place the food over an unlit burner. If your grill has just two burners, turn off the one toward the back of the grill. If your grill has more than two burners, turn off the one(s) in the middle of the grill. The burners that are left on can be set to high, medium, or low heat, as desired. Whenever the food is over an unlit burner and the lid is closed, you're grilling over indirect heat.

SETTING UP YOUR GAS GRILL FOR DIRECT AND INDIRECT COOKING

There's nothing complicated about lighting a gas grill. However, gas grill operation does vary, so be sure to consult the owner's manual that came with your grill. To light a Weber® gas grill, first open the lid so unlit gas fumes don't collect in the cooking box. Next, slowly open the valve on your propane tank (or natural gas line) all the way and wait a minute for the gas to travel through the gas line. Then turn on the burners, setting them all to high. Close the lid and preheat the grill for 10 to 15 minutes. Then simply leave all the burners on and adjust them for the heat level you want.

If you smell gas, turn off all the burners. Close the valve on your propane tank (or natural gas line) and disconnect the hose. Wait a

Grilling Fundamentals

ESSENTIAL TOOLS FOR THE GRILLER

TONGS

Definitely the hardest working tool of all. You will need three pairs: one for raw food, one for cooked food, and one for arranging charcoal.

GRILL BRUSH

Spring for a solid, long-handled model with stainless steel bristles. Use it to clean off the cooking grates before and during grilling.

GRILL PAN

Here's a great tool for grilling small foods that might otherwise fall through the cooking grates, like mushrooms and cherry tomatoes. Be sure to preheat the pan before the food goes on.

CHIMNEY STARTER

This is the simplest tool for starting lump charcoal or briquettes faster and more evenly than you could with lighter fluid. Look for one with a capacity of at least 5 quarts.

INSTANT-READ THERMOMETER

This little gadget could save you from overcooking your steaks. Coming in at the side of each steak, insert the probe in the center of the thickest part of the meat and avoid touching any bone, because the bone conducts heat.

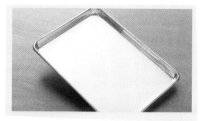

SHEET PAN

A baking sheet like this one does a lot more than bake. It is a great portable work surface for oiling and seasoning foods, and there's nothing better to use as a landing pad for steaks coming off the grill.

BARBECUE MITTS

Protect your hand and forearm when managing a charcoal fire or reaching toward the back of a hot grill.

SPATULA

Look for a long-handled spatula designed with a bent (offset) neck so that the blade is set lower than the handle. It's a good alternative to tongs for flipping steaks and other foods.

BASTING BRUSH

A good brush is always helpful for oiling your steaks and applying your glazes and sauces. Today's brushes with stainless steel handles and silicon bristles can go right into the dishwasher.

TIMER

As the old saying goes, timing is everything … that and temperature, because every great steak depends on the right combination of timing and temperature.

14

RIB-EYE

16 Bone-in Rib-Eye Steaks with Sweet, Pan-Roasted Garlic
18 Big Cowboy Steaks with Whiskey Barbecue Sauce
20 Rib-Eye Steaks with Tomato-Curry Sauce
21 Rib-Eye Steaks with Red Wine Sauce
22 Philly-Style Steak Sandwiches
    with Grilled Onions and Provolone
24 Straight-Shootin' Cowboy Steaks with Toasted Cumin Rub
25 Market Steaks with Bourbon Barbecue Sauce
26 Rib-Eye Steaks with Chipotle Butter
28 Rib-Eye Steaks with Tomato-Chimichurri Sauce

STRIP

30 Strip Steaks with Mushrooms, Bacon, and Blue Cheese
32 New York Steaks with Toasted Fennel Spice Rub
33 Mesquite-Grilled Strip Steaks with Worcestershire Paste
34 Steak House Salad with Blue Cheese Vinaigrette
36 Chicago Strip Steaks with Creamy Mustard Sauce
37 Ambassador Steaks with French Roast Spice Rub
38 New York Strip Steaks with Basil-Arugula Pesto
40 New York Strip Steaks with Zesty Red Barbecue Sauce
41 Thai Rice Bowl with Lemongrass-Marinated Steak
42 Steak and Eggs with Gremolata

FILET MIGNON

44 Filet Mignon Steaks with Crab Guacamole
46 Mexican Tenderloin Strips with Avocado, Cheese,
    and Warm Tortillas
47 Filet Mignon Steaks with Orange, Hoisin, and Ginger Sauce
48 Filet Mignon Steaks with Garlicky Shrimp
50 Pepper-Crusted Filet Mignon Steaks
    with Lemon-Parsley Butter
51 Filet Mignon Steaks with Black Olive Pesto
52 Filet Mignon Crostini with Balsamic Onion Jam

T-BONE

54 T-Bone Steaks with Horseradish-Lemon Cream Sauce
56 Really Thick T-Bones with Creamy White Beans
57 Rancho T-Bones with Red Chile-Honey Glaze
58 Argentinean-Style T-Bone Steaks with Salsa Criolla

PORTERHOUSE

60 Ginger Porterhouse Steaks with Roasted Sesame Salt
62 Porterhouse Steaks with Herbed Vinaigrette
63 Porterhouse Steaks with Spice Crust and Garlic Butter
64 Porterhouse Steaks with Béarnaise Sauce

FLANK

66 Pacific Rim Flank Steak with Vegetable Medley
67 Steak and Tomato Wraps with Avocado Sauce
68 Tagliata of Flank Steak with Arugula and Shaved Parmesan
70 Flank Steak Satay with Peanut Sauce
71 Flank Steak Gyros with Fresh Cucumber Salad
72 Steak Tacos with Grilled Tomatillo Salsa
74 Marinated Flank Steak with Creole Flavors
75 Flank Steak Marinated in Teriyaki and Bourbon
76 Italian Beef Sandwiches with Pickled Vegetables

SKIRT

77 Skirt Steak Fajitas with Jalapeño Salsa
78 Balsamic-Marinated Skirt Steaks
    with Grilled Smashed Potatoes and Olive Aioli
80 Steak and Spinach Salad with Sesame-Ginger Dressing
81 Rosemary-Garlic Skirt Steaks with Shiitake Mushrooms
82 Skirt Steaks with Poblano and Cherry Tomato Salsa

TOP SIRLOIN

84 Top Sirloin Steak with Santa Fe Spice Rub
85 Sirloin Steak Marinated in Curry and Coconut
86 Teriyaki Sirloin Kabobs with Bell Peppers and Pineapple
88 Sirloin and Cherry Tomato Kabobs with Creamy Polenta
90 Peruvian Sirloin Skewers with Peppers and Onions
91 Spanish Sirloin Steak with Horseradish-Tarragon Sauce
92 Sirloin Steaks with Wasabi-Garlic Sauce

TRI-TIP

94 Tri-Tip Steak Sandwiches with Whole-Grain Mustard Sauce
96 Peppered Tri-Tip with Roasted Peperonata
97 Hickory Tri-Tip Steak with Chive Cream Sauce
98 Tri-Tip and Zucchini Skewers with Smoked Paprika Aioli

FLATIRON

100 Flatiron Steaks with Herb Butter and Grilled Broccolini
102 Citrus-Marinated Flatiron Kabobs with Scallions
103 Flatiron Steak Burritos with Black Bean Salsa
104 Miso-Marinated Flatiron Steaks with Shiitake Mushrooms

CHUCK

106 Easy Chuck Steak Sandwiches with Sweet Chili Sauce

HANGER

107 Hanger Steaks with Butcher's Big Red Sauce
108 Hanger Steaks with Gruyère-Shallot Fondue

BONE-IN RIB-EYE STEAKS
WITH SWEET, PAN-ROASTED GARLIC

PREP TIME: 10 minutes, plus about 20 minutes for the garlic
GRILLING TIME: 6 to 8 minutes

25 garlic cloves, peeled
⅛ teaspoon crushed red pepper flakes
½–1 cup extra-virgin olive oil

4 bone-in rib-eye steaks, each 10 to 12 ounces and about 1 inch thick, trimmed of excess fat
Sea salt
Ground black pepper

1. In a small saucepan over low heat, combine the garlic and red pepper flakes with ½ to 1 cup of oil, making sure you have enough oil to cover the garlic cloves. Cook at a low simmer until the garlic starts to brown, about 20 minutes. Remove the pan from the heat and allow the garlic to cool in the oil. The garlic will continue to soften and brown until the oil cools. Set aside.

2. Pour ¼ cup of the garlic oil onto a sheet pan. Dredge the steaks through the oil, coating both sides. Season evenly with salt and pepper. Allow the steaks to stand at room temperature for 15 to 30 minutes before grilling.

3. Prepare the grill for direct cooking over high heat (450° to 550°F).

4. Brush the cooking grates clean. Grill the steaks over *direct high heat*, with the lid closed as much as possible, until cooked to your desired doneness, 6 to 8 minutes for medium rare, turning once or twice (if flare-ups occur, move the steaks temporarily over indirect heat). Remove from the grill and let rest for 3 to 5 minutes.

5. Serve the steaks warm, topped with a generous sprinkling of salt and some garlic. Spoon some of the garlic oil over the steaks, if desired. Serving suggestion: Asparagus with Sherry-Bacon Vinaigrette (for recipe, see page 113).

SERVES: 4

BIG COWBOY STEAKS
WITH WHISKEY BARBECUE SAUCE

PREP TIME: 5 minutes, plus about 15 minutes for the sauce
GRILLING TIME: 8 to 10 minutes

Sauce

- 2 tablespoons extra-virgin olive oil
- 1 cup finely chopped yellow onion
- 1 tablespoon finely chopped garlic
- ¼ cup whiskey
- 3 tablespoons tomato paste
- ½ cup pure maple syrup
- 1 tablespoon cider vinegar
- 2 teaspoons Dijon mustard
- 1 teaspoon smoked paprika
- 1 teaspoon Tabasco® sauce
- ½ teaspoon ground black pepper

- 4 bone-in rib-eye steaks, each 14 to 16 ounces and about 1¼ inches thick, trimmed of excess fat
  Extra-virgin olive oil
  Kosher salt
  Ground black pepper

1. In a large saucepan over medium-high heat, warm the oil. Add the onion and cook until it is tender but not browned, 5 to 7 minutes, stirring occasionally. Add the garlic and cook until fragrant, about 1 minute, stirring constantly to prevent browning. Remove the pan from the heat and slowly pour in the whiskey (beware of any flames). Return the pan to the heat and cook until the whiskey has almost completely evaporated, about 2 minutes. Stir in the tomato paste until well incorporated. Add the syrup, vinegar, mustard, paprika, Tabasco, and pepper, and simmer for 2 to 3 minutes, to meld the flavors and thicken the sauce slightly. Remove from the heat and set aside.

2. Lightly brush the steaks on both sides with oil and season evenly with salt and pepper. Allow the steaks to stand at room temperature for 15 to 30 minutes before grilling.

3. Prepare the grill for direct cooking over high heat (450° to 550°F).

4. Brush the cooking grates clean. Grill the steaks over **direct high heat**, with the lid closed as much as possible, until cooked to your desired doneness, 8 to 10 minutes for medium rare, turning once or twice (if flare-ups occur, move the steaks temporarily over indirect heat). Remove from the grill and let rest for 3 to 5 minutes. Serve warm with the sauce.

SERVES: 4 to 6

RIB-EYE STEAKS
WITH TOMATO-CURRY SAUCE

PREP TIME: 20 minutes
GRILLING TIME: 6 to 8 minutes

Sauce

- 1 tablespoon vegetable oil
- 1 teaspoon minced garlic
- ½ teaspoon red curry paste
- 1 cup tomato sauce
- 1 can (5.5 ounces) unsweetened coconut milk, stirred
- ¼ teaspoon kosher salt
- ¼ teaspoon ground black pepper
- 2 tablespoons finely chopped fresh basil leaves

- 4 rib-eye steaks, each 10 to 12 ounces and about 1 inch thick, trimmed of excess fat
  Vegetable oil
- 2 teaspoons kosher salt
- 1 teaspoon ground black pepper
- 2 tablespoons finely chopped fresh basil or mint leaves (optional)

1. In a medium saucepan over medium heat, warm the oil. Add the garlic and curry paste, stirring immediately to break apart the paste. After about 1 minute, add all the remaining sauce ingredients, except the basil, and stir. Bring the sauce to a simmer. Cook until the mixture reaches a cream sauce consistency, about 5 minutes, stirring occasionally. Add the basil during the last minute. Remove the sauce from the heat.

2. Brush the steaks on both sides with oil and season evenly with the salt and pepper. Allow the steaks to stand at room temperature for 15 to 30 minutes before grilling.

3. Prepare the grill for direct cooking over high heat (450° to 550°F).

4. Brush the cooking grates clean. Grill the steaks over ***direct high heat***, with the lid closed as much as possible, until cooked to your desired doneness, 6 to 8 minutes for medium rare, turning once or twice (if flare-ups occur, move the steaks temporarily over indirect heat). Remove from the grill, brush both sides with a little sauce, and let rest for 3 to 5 minutes. While the steaks rest, reheat the sauce over medium heat.

5. Cut the steaks into slices. Pour some sauce in a pool on individual plates (you may not need all of the sauce) and then arrange the slices of steak on top. If desired, garnish with basil or mint.

SERVES: 4 to 6

RIB-EYE STEAKS
WITH RED WINE SAUCE

PREP TIME: 5 minutes, plus about 25 minutes for the sauce
GRILLING TIME: 6 to 8 minutes

Sauce
2 tablespoons minced shallot
1½ cups dry red wine
1 tablespoon tomato paste
2 teaspoons balsamic vinegar
½ teaspoon Worcestershire sauce
3 tablespoons butter, cut into 3 pieces
   Kosher salt
   Ground black pepper

4 rib-eye steaks, each about 8 ounces and 1 inch thick, trimmed of excess fat
   Extra-virgin olive oil
1 tablespoon kosher salt
1 teaspoon ground black pepper

1. In a medium saucepan over high heat, bring the shallot and wine to a boil. Then immediately reduce the heat to medium and simmer until the wine has reduced to about ½ cup, 15 to 20 minutes. Add the tomato paste, vinegar, and Worcestershire sauce. Remove from the heat and add the butter piece by piece, whisking to incorporate the butter into the sauce. Season with salt and pepper.

2. Lightly brush the steaks on both sides with oil and season evenly with the salt and pepper. Allow the steaks to stand at room temperature for 15 to 30 minutes before grilling.

3. Prepare the grill for direct cooking over high heat (450° to 550°F).

4. Brush the cooking grates clean. Grill the steaks over **_direct high heat_**, with the lid closed as much as possible, until cooked to your desired doneness, 6 to 8 minutes for medium rare, turning once or twice (if flare-ups occur, move the steaks temporarily over indirect heat). Remove from the grill and let rest for 3 to 5 minutes. While the steaks rest, reheat the sauce over medium heat. Serve the steaks warm with the sauce. Serving suggestion: Grilled Garlic Bread (for recipe, see page 125).

SERVES: 4

PHILLY-STYLE STEAK SANDWICHES
WITH GRILLED ONIONS AND PROVOLONE

PREP TIME: 20 minutes
GRILLING TIME: 11 to 13 minutes
SPECIAL EQUIPMENT: perforated grill pan

1 large yellow onion, thinly sliced
1 red bell pepper, thinly sliced
1 yellow bell pepper, thinly sliced
2 garlic cloves, thinly sliced
2 tablespoons extra-virgin olive oil
1 teaspoon dried oregano
  Kosher salt
  Ground black pepper

2 boneless rib-eye steaks, each about 8 ounces
  and 1 inch thick, trimmed of excess fat
  Extra-virgin olive oil
4 ciabatta rolls, split
1 garlic clove, peeled
8 thin slices provolone cheese, about 1 ounce each

TIP!

In order to cut the meat easily into thin slices, firm it up first by placing it (wrapped in plastic) in the freezer for about 30 minutes.

1. Prepare the grill for direct cooking over high heat (450° to 550°F) and preheat the grill pan.

2. In a large bowl combine the onion, peppers, garlic, oil, and oregano. Season with salt and pepper and toss to coat evenly. Spread the vegetables on the grill pan in a single layer. Grill over *direct high heat*, with the lid closed as much as possible, until they start to brown and are tender, about 6 minutes, stirring occasionally. Transfer to a medium bowl.

3. Cut the steaks lengthwise into ⅛-inch slices. Place the slices in a medium bowl, add just enough oil to coat them lightly, and season with salt and pepper; toss to coat. Grill the steak slices on the grill pan over *direct high heat*, with the lid closed as much as possible, until the meat begins to curl and brown, 4 to 6 minutes, turning occasionally. Wearing barbecue mitts, remove the pan from the grill and set it down on a heat-proof surface.

4. Brush the cooking grates clean. Lightly brush the cut sides of the rolls with oil and grill them over *direct high heat* until toasted, 30 seconds to 1 minute. Gently rub the garlic onto the toasted rolls.

5. Build the sandwiches with cheese, meat, onions, and peppers. Serve warm.

SERVES: 4

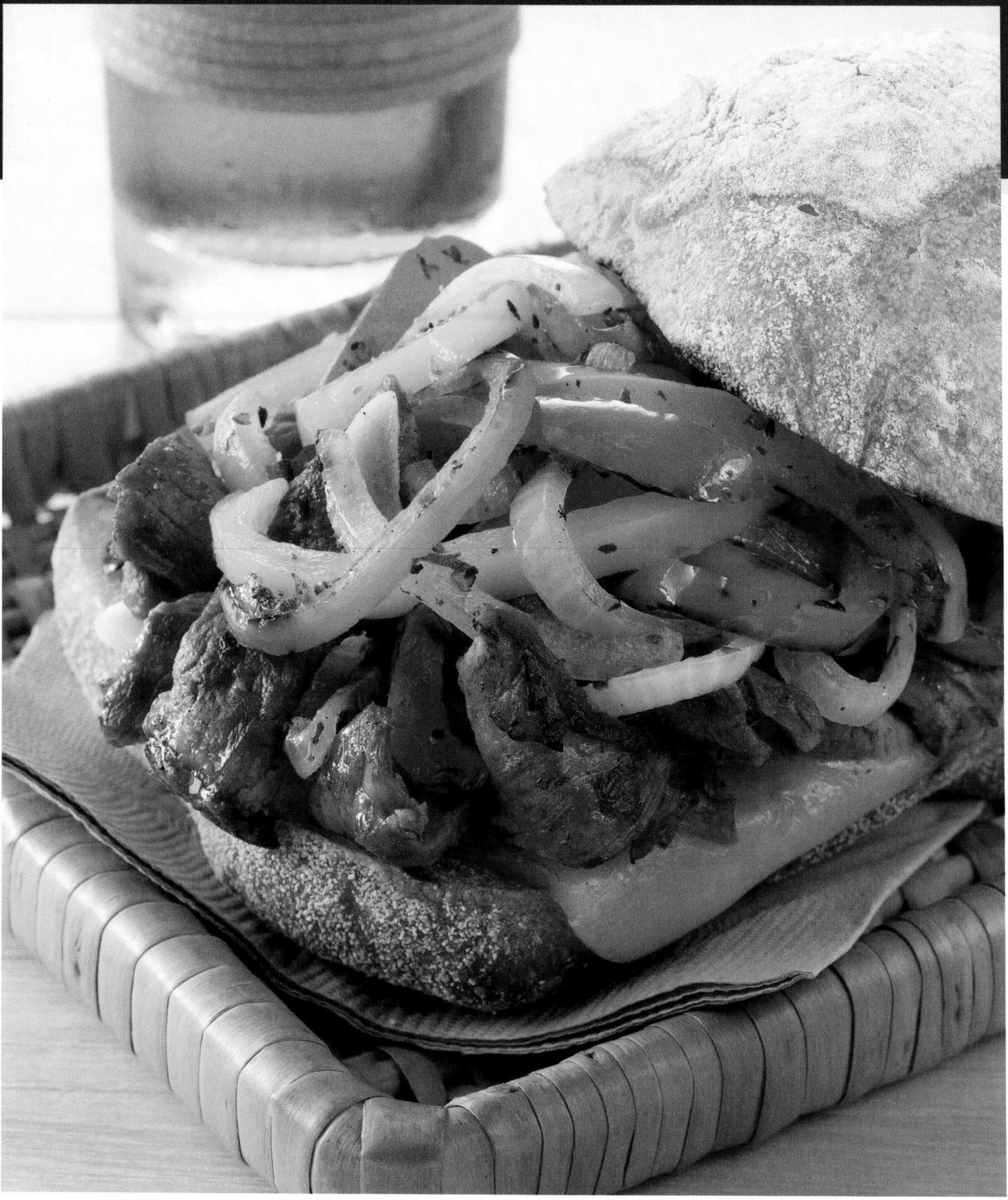

STRAIGHT-SHOOTIN' COWBOY STEAKS
WITH TOASTED CUMIN RUB

PREP TIME: 10 minutes
GRILLING TIME: 6 to 8 minutes
SPECIAL EQUIPMENT: spice mill

Rub

- 2 teaspoons cumin seed
- 1 teaspoon mustard seed
- 1 teaspoon coriander seed
- 2 teaspoons paprika
- 2 teaspoons kosher salt
- 2 teaspoons brown sugar
- ½ teaspoon granulated garlic
- ½ teaspoon ground cayenne pepper

- 4 bone-in rib-eye steaks, each 10 to 12 ounces and about 1 inch thick, trimmed of excess fat
  Extra-virgin olive oil
  Sea salt

1. In a medium skillet over medium-high heat, toast the cumin, mustard, and coriander seeds until fragrant, 2 to 3 minutes, shaking the pan occasionally. Transfer the seeds to a spice mill. Add the remaining rub ingredients and pulse until finely ground.

2. Lightly coat the steaks on both sides with oil and season evenly with the rub. Allow the steaks to stand at room temperature for 15 to 30 minutes before grilling.

3. Prepare the grill for direct cooking over high heat (450° to 550°F).

4. Brush the cooking grates clean. Grill the steaks over **direct high heat**, with the lid closed as much as possible, until cooked to your desired doneness, 6 to 8 minutes for medium rare, turning once or twice (if flare-ups occur, move the steaks temporarily over indirect heat). Remove from the grill and let rest for 3 to 5 minutes. Season with salt and serve warm. Serving suggestion: Roasted Corn and Black Bean Salad (for recipe, see page 121).

SERVES: 4

MARKET STEAKS
WITH BOURBON BARBECUE SAUCE

PREP TIME: 15 minutes, plus about 25 minutes for the sauce
MARINATING TIME: 45 minutes to 4 hours
GRILLING TIME: 6 to 8 minutes

Marinade
½ cup bourbon
½ cup packed brown sugar
⅓ cup soy sauce
⅓ cup fresh lemon juice
2 tablespoons Worcestershire sauce
2 teaspoons finely chopped garlic
2 teaspoons finely chopped fresh thyme leaves

4 rib-eye steaks (also called market steaks), each 10 to 12 ounces and about 1 inch thick, trimmed of excess fat

Sauce
Extra-virgin olive oil
¼ cup finely chopped yellow onion
2 teaspoons minced garlic
1¼ cups ketchup
⅓ cup bourbon
¼ cup light molasses
3 tablespoons Dijon mustard
3 tablespoons water
2 tablespoons Worcestershire sauce
2 teaspoons hot chili-garlic sauce, such as Sriracha
1 teaspoon paprika

1. In a medium bowl whisk the marinade ingredients. Place the steaks in a large, resealable plastic bag and pour in the marinade. Press the air out of the bag and seal tightly. Turn the bag to distribute the marinade, and refrigerate for 45 minutes to 4 hours, turning the bag once or twice.

2. Allow the steaks to stand at room temperature for 15 to 30 minutes before grilling.

3. Prepare the grill for direct cooking over high heat (450° to 550°F).

4. In a heavy-bottomed saucepan over medium heat, warm 2 tablespoons of oil. Add the onion and cook until tender, about 3 minutes, stirring occasionally. Add the garlic and cook just until fragrant, about 30 seconds. Add the remaining sauce ingredients and bring to a simmer. Reduce the heat to low and continue cooking for about 15 minutes, stirring frequently to prevent scorching. Remove the sauce from the heat.

5. Remove the steaks from the bag and discard the marinade. Pat the steaks dry with paper towels. Brush both sides of each steak with oil.

6. Brush the cooking grates clean. Grill the steaks over ***direct high heat***, with the lid closed as much as possible, until cooked to your desired doneness, 6 to 8 minutes for medium rare, turning once or twice (if flare-ups occur, move the steaks temporarily over indirect heat). Remove from the grill and let rest for 3 to 5 minutes. Serve the steaks warm with the sauce.

SERVES: 4

RIB-EYE STEAKS
WITH CHIPOTLE BUTTER

PREP TIME: 15 minutes
GRILLING TIME: 6 to 8 minutes

Butter
- ¼ cup (½ stick) unsalted butter, softened
- 1 tablespoon minced canned chipotle chiles in adobo
- 1 teaspoon brown sugar
- ¼ teaspoon kosher salt

Rub
- 2 teaspoons kosher salt
- 1½ teaspoons ancho chile powder
- 1 teaspoon unsweetened cocoa powder
- ½ teaspoon ground black pepper
- ½ teaspoon brown sugar

- 4 rib-eye steaks, each about 10 ounces and 1 inch thick, trimmed of excess fat
  Extra-virgin olive oil

1. In a medium bowl mix the butter ingredients until evenly incorporated.

2. Prepare the grill for direct cooking over high heat (450° to 550°F).

3. In a small bowl combine the rub ingredients. Lightly brush the steaks on both sides with oil and season evenly with the rub, gently pressing the rub into the meat. Allow the steaks to stand at room temperature for 15 to 30 minutes before grilling.

4. Brush the cooking grates clean. Grill the steaks over **direct high heat**, with the lid closed as much as possible, until cooked to your desired doneness, 6 to 8 minutes for medium rare, turning once or twice (if flare-ups occur, move the steaks temporarily over indirect heat). Remove from the grill and smear the butter on top. Let rest for 3 to 5 minutes. Serve warm.

SERVES: 4

RIB-EYE STEAKS
WITH TOMATO-CHIMICHURRI SAUCE

PREP TIME: 20 minutes
GRILLING TIME: 6 to 8 minutes

Sauce

- 1 cup loosely packed fresh Italian parsley leaves and tender stems
- ½ cup extra-virgin olive oil
- ⅓ cup loosely packed fresh cilantro leaves
- ¼ cup oil-packed sun-dried tomatoes, drained
- 3 garlic cloves
- ¾ teaspoon crushed red pepper flakes
  Kosher salt
  Ground black pepper

Rub

- 1 tablespoon ground cumin
- 1 tablespoon ground coriander
- 2 teaspoons kosher salt
- ¼ teaspoon ground black pepper

- 4 rib-eye steaks, each about 12 ounces and 1 inch thick, trimmed of excess fat
  Extra-virgin olive oil

1. In a food processor combine the sauce ingredients. Pulse until you get a semi-smooth consistency. Season with salt and pepper. Transfer to a small bowl and set aside.

2. In a small bowl mix the rub ingredients. Lightly brush the steaks on both sides with oil and season evenly with the rub. Allow the steaks to stand at room temperature for 15 to 30 minutes before grilling.

3. Prepare the grill for direct cooking over high heat (450° to 550°F).

4. Brush the cooking grates clean. Grill the steaks over ***direct high heat***, with the lid closed as much as possible, until cooked to your desired doneness, 6 to 8 minutes for medium rare, turning once or twice (if flare-ups occur, move the steaks temporarily over indirect heat). Remove from the grill and let rest for 3 to 5 minutes. Serve warm with the sauce.

SERVES: 4

STRIP STEAKS
WITH MUSHROOMS, BACON, AND BLUE CHEESE

PREP TIME: 30 minutes
MARINATING TIME: 30 minutes to 1 hour
GRILLING TIME: 14 to 20 minutes

Marinade
- ½ cup dry sherry
- 2 tablespoons extra-virgin olive oil
- 2 tablespoons soy sauce
- ¼ teaspoon ground black pepper

Relish
- 3 large portabello mushrooms, cleaned, stems and black gills removed
- 1 small yellow onion, cut crosswise into ¼-inch slices
- 4 slices thick-cut smoked bacon, cooked and coarsely chopped
- 1 teaspoon finely chopped fresh thyme leaves
- ¼ cup finely chopped fresh Italian parsley leaves
- ¼ cup crumbled Gorgonzola cheese
  Kosher salt
  Ground black pepper

- 6 New York strip steaks, each about 12 ounces and 1 inch thick, trimmed of excess fat
  Extra-virgin olive oil

1. In a large bowl whisk the marinade ingredients. Add the mushrooms and onion slices and turn to coat. Marinate at room temperature for at least 30 minutes or up to 1 hour, turning occasionally.

2. Prepare the grill for direct cooking over medium heat (350° to 450°F).

3. Brush the cooking grates clean. Grill the mushroom caps, gill sides down first, over *direct medium heat*, with the lid closed as much as possible, until cooked through, 8 to 12 minutes, turning once and brushing occasionally with the marinade. At the same time, grill the onion slices until softened and beginning to char, 6 to 8 minutes, turning once.

4. Chop the mushrooms and onions and place in a medium bowl. Gently stir in the bacon, thyme, parsley, and cheese. Season with salt and pepper.

5. Lightly brush the steaks with oil and season with salt and pepper. Allow the steaks to stand at room temperature for 15 to 30 minutes before grilling.

6. Increase the temperature of the grill to high heat (450° to 550°F). Grill the steaks over *direct high heat*, with the lid closed as much as possible, until cooked to your desired doneness, 6 to 8 minutes for medium rare, turning once or twice (if flare-ups occur, move the steaks temporarily over indirect heat). Remove from the grill and let rest for 3 to 5 minutes. Serve warm with the relish. Serving suggestion: Corn on the Cob with Basil-Parmesan Butter (for recipe, see page 120).

SERVES: 6

NEW YORK STEAKS
WITH TOASTED FENNEL SPICE RUB

PREP TIME: 10 minutes
GRILLING TIME: 6 to 8 minutes
SPECIAL EQUIPMENT: spice mill

Rub

- 1 tablespoon fennel seed
- 1 tablespoon black peppercorns
- 2 teaspoons mustard seed
- 1 teaspoon cumin seed
- 1 teaspoon kosher salt
- ½ teaspoon granulated garlic

- 4 New York strip steaks, each 8 to 10 ounces and about 1 inch thick, trimmed of excess fat
  Extra-virgin olive oil
  Sea salt

1. In a medium skillet over medium-high heat, toast the fennel seed, peppercorns, mustard seed, and cumin seed until the spices release their fragrance, 2 to 3 minutes, shaking the pan occasionally. Transfer the spices to a spice mill, add the remaining rub ingredients, and coarsely grind the spices.

2. Brush the steaks on both sides with oil and season with the rub, pressing the spices into the meat. Allow the steaks to stand at room temperature for 15 to 30 minutes before grilling.

3. Prepare the grill for direct cooking over high heat (450° to 550°F).

4. Brush the cooking grates clean. Grill the steaks over *direct high heat*, with the lid closed as much as possible, until cooked to your desired doneness, 6 to 8 minutes for medium rare, turning once or twice (if flare-ups occur, move the steaks temporarily over indirect heat). Remove from the grill and let rest for 3 to 5 minutes. Season with salt and serve warm. Serving suggestion: Grilled Carrots (for recipe, see page 117).

SERVES: 4

MESQUITE-GRILLED STRIP STEAKS
WITH WORCESTERSHIRE PASTE

PREP TIME: 10 minutes
GRILLING TIME: 6 to 8 minutes

Paste

- 2 tablespoons extra-virgin olive oil
- 2 tablespoons Worcestershire sauce
- 2 teaspoons cracked black pepper
- 2 teaspoons granulated garlic
- 1½ teaspoons kosher salt
- 1 teaspoon smoked paprika
- 1 teaspoon ground cumin
- ½ teaspoon ground cinnamon

- 4 New York strip steaks, each 10 to 12 ounces and about 1 inch thick, trimmed of excess fat

- 2 handfuls mesquite wood chips, soaked in water for at least 30 minutes

1. In a small bowl mix the paste ingredients. Spread the paste evenly over the steaks, and allow the steaks to stand at room temperature for 15 to 30 minutes before grilling.

2. Prepare the grill for direct cooking over high heat (450° to 550°F).

3. Brush the cooking grates clean. Drain and add the wood chips directly onto burning coals or to the smoker box of a gas grill, following manufacturer's instructions. When the wood chips begin to generate a good amount of smoke, place the steaks over **direct high heat**, close the lid, and cook to your desired doneness, 6 to 8 minutes for medium rare, turning once or twice (if flare-ups occur, move the steaks temporarily over indirect heat). Remove from the grill and let rest for 3 to 5 minutes. Serve warm. Serving suggestion: Smoky Sweet Baked Beans (for recipe, see page 125).

SERVES: 4

STEAK HOUSE SALAD
WITH BLUE CHEESE VINAIGRETTE

PREP TIME: 15 minutes
GRILLING TIME: 6 to 8 minutes

Salad

 3 romaine lettuce hearts, halved, cored, and
     coarsely chopped
 1 pint cherry tomatoes, each one halved
 ½ cup fresh Italian parsley leaves
 ½ red onion, sliced into paper-thin half-moons

 4 New York strip steaks, each 10 to 12 ounces and
     about 1 inch thick, trimmed of excess fat
     Extra-virgin olive oil
     Kosher salt
     Ground black pepper

Vinaigrette

 ½ cup extra-virgin olive oil
 ⅓ cup crumbled blue cheese
 ¼ cup red wine vinegar
 1 teaspoon kosher salt
 ½ teaspoon ground black pepper

1. In a large bowl combine the salad ingredients.

2. Lightly brush the steaks on both sides with oil and season evenly with salt and pepper. Allow the steaks to stand at room temperature for 15 to 30 minutes before grilling.

3. Prepare the grill for direct cooking over high heat (450° to 550°F).

4. Brush the cooking grates clean. Grill the steaks over ***direct high heat***, with the lid closed as much as possible, until cooked to your desired doneness, 6 to 8 minutes for medium rare, turning once or twice (if flare-ups occur, move the steaks temporarily over indirect heat). Transfer the steaks to a cutting board and let rest for 3 to 5 minutes.

5. While the steaks rest, whisk the vinaigrette ingredients in a small bowl. Drizzle the salad with the vinaigrette and toss to coat. Divide the salad evenly among individual serving plates.

6. Cut the steaks into thin slices. Pile steak on top of each salad and serve with any remaining dressing.

SERVES: 6 to 8

CHICAGO STRIP STEAKS
WITH CREAMY MUSTARD SAUCE

PREP TIME: 5 minutes, plus about 10 minutes for the sauce
GRILLING TIME: 6 to 8 minutes

6 New York strip steaks, each 10 to 12 ounces and about 1 inch thick, trimmed of excess fat
Extra-virgin olive oil
2 tablespoons Weber® Chicago Steak™ Seasoning

Sauce

1 tablespoon unsalted butter
2 tablespoons minced shallot
2 tablespoons cognac or brandy (optional)
½ cup low-sodium beef broth
¾ cup heavy cream
3 tablespoons whole-grain mustard
Kosher salt

1. Lightly coat the steaks on both sides with oil and sprinkle evenly with the steak seasoning. Allow the steaks to stand at room temperature for 15 to 30 minutes before grilling.

2. Prepare the grill for direct cooking over high heat (450° to 550°F).

3. In a medium skillet over medium heat, melt the butter. Add the shallot and cook until softened, 1 to 2 minutes, stirring often. If using, add the cognac and cook until reduced to a glaze, about 30 seconds. Add the broth and bring to a boil over high heat. Cook until the stock reduces by half, 2 to 3 minutes. Add the cream and bring to a simmer (not a boil). Whisk in the mustard and simmer until the sauce is reduced to ¾ cup and is thick enough to coat the back of a spoon, 3 to 5 minutes longer. Season with salt. Set the skillet aside.

4. Brush the cooking grates clean. Grill the steaks over **direct high heat**, with the lid closed as much as possible, until cooked to your desired doneness, 6 to 8 minutes for medium rare, turning once or twice (if flare-ups occur, move the steaks temporarily over indirect heat). Remove from the grill and let rest for 3 to 5 minutes.

5. While the steaks rest, reheat the sauce over low heat. Place each steak on an individual plate. Spoon the sauce over the top. Serve warm.

SERVES: 6

AMBASSADOR STEAKS
WITH FRENCH ROAST SPICE RUB

PREP TIME: 5 minutes
GRILLING TIME: 8 to 10 minutes

Rub

- 2 tablespoons coarsely ground French roast coffee beans
- 2 teaspoons kosher salt
- 1 teaspoon light brown sugar
- ¾ teaspoon ground black pepper
- ½ teaspoon granulated garlic

- 4 New York strip steaks (also called ambassador steaks), each 8 to 10 ounces and about 1¼ inches thick, trimmed of excess fat
  Extra-virgin olive oil

1. In a small bowl mix the rub ingredients.

2. Lightly brush the steaks on both sides with oil and season evenly with the rub. Allow the steaks to stand at room temperature for 15 to 30 minutes before grilling.

3. Prepare the grill for direct cooking over high heat (450° to 550°F).

4. Brush the cooking grates clean. Grill the steaks over **_direct high heat_**, with the lid closed as much as possible, until cooked to your desired doneness, 8 to 10 minutes for medium rare, turning once or twice (if flare-ups occur, move the steaks temporarily over indirect heat). Remove from the grill and let the steaks rest for 3 to 5 minutes. Serve warm. Serving suggestion: Corn on the Cob with Basil-Parmesan Butter (for recipe, see page 120).

SERVES: 4

NEW YORK STRIP STEAKS
WITH BASIL-ARUGULA PESTO

PREP TIME: 15 minutes
GRILLING TIME: 6 to 8 minutes

Pesto

1½ cups loosely packed baby arugula
½ cup loosely packed fresh basil leaves
2 tablespoons roughly chopped toasted walnuts
1 garlic clove
½ teaspoon finely grated lemon zest
    Extra-virgin olive oil
    Kosher salt
    Ground black pepper

6 New York strip steaks, each 8 to 10 ounces and about 1 inch thick, trimmed of excess fat

1. In the bowl of a food processor combine the arugula, basil, walnuts, garlic, and lemon zest, and pulse until coarsely chopped. With the machine running, gradually add ¼ cup oil and process until well blended. Season with salt and pepper.

2. Lightly brush the steaks on both sides with oil and season evenly with salt and pepper. Allow the steaks to stand at room temperature for 15 to 30 minutes before grilling.

3. Prepare the grill for direct cooking over high heat (450° to 550°F).

4. Brush the cooking grates clean. Grill the steaks over ***direct high heat***, with the lid closed as much as possible, until cooked to your desired doneness, 6 to 8 minutes for medium rare, turning once or twice (if flare-ups occur, move the steaks temporarily over indirect heat). Remove from the grill and let rest for 3 to 5 minutes. Serve warm with a generous dollop of pesto on top of each steak. Serving suggestion: Corn and Tomato Summer Salad (for recipe, see page 121).

SERVES: 6

NEW YORK STRIP STEAKS
WITH ZESTY RED BARBECUE SAUCE

PREP TIME: 10 minutes, plus about 10 minutes for the sauce
GRILLING TIME: 6 to 8 minutes
SPECIAL EQUIPMENT: spice mill

Rub

- 1 tablespoon black peppercorns
- 1 teaspoon prepared chili powder
- 1 teaspoon kosher salt
- 1 teaspoon brown sugar
- ¼ teaspoon granulated garlic
- ¼ teaspoon granulated onion

Sauce

- ½ cup ketchup
- ¼ cup water
- 1 tablespoon Worcestershire sauce
- 1 tablespoon red wine vinegar
- 1 teaspoon light brown sugar
- 1 teaspoon prepared chili powder
- 1 teaspoon granulated onion
- ¼ teaspoon ground black pepper

- 4 New York strip steaks, each 10 to 12 ounces and about 1 inch thick, trimmed of excess fat
  Extra-virgin olive oil

1. Crush the peppercorns in a spice mill. Transfer to a small bowl and combine with the rest of the rub ingredients.

2. In a small saucepan whisk the sauce ingredients. Simmer over low heat for about 10 minutes to allow the sugar to fully dissolve and all of the flavors to blend, stirring occasionally. Set aside.

3. Lightly brush the steaks on both sides with oil and season evenly with the rub. Allow the steaks to stand at room temperature for 15 to 30 minutes before grilling.

4. Prepare the grill for direct cooking over high heat (450° to 550°F).

5. Brush the cooking grates clean. Grill the steaks over ***direct high heat***, with the lid closed as much as possible, until cooked to your desired doneness, 6 to 8 minutes for medium rare, turning once or twice (if flare-ups occur, move the steaks temporarily over indirect heat). Remove from the grill and let rest for 3 to 5 minutes. Serve warm with the sauce on the side. Serving suggestion: Skillet Corn Bread with Bacon and Chives (for recipe, see page 124).

SERVES: 4

THAI RICE BOWL
WITH LEMONGRASS-MARINATED STEAK

PREP TIME: 40 minutes, plus time to cook the rice
MARINATING TIME: 1 to 2 hours
GRILLING TIME: 4 to 6 minutes

Marinade
- ¾ cup finely chopped fresh lemongrass
- 2 tablespoons fish sauce
- 2 tablespoons soy sauce
- 6 garlic cloves, finely chopped
- 1 tablespoon granulated sugar
- 1 tablespoon toasted sesame oil

- 4 New York strip steaks, each about 6 ounces and ¾ inch thick, trimmed of excess fat

Dressing
- ⅓ cup fish sauce
- ⅓ cup fresh lime juice
- 2 tablespoons granulated sugar
- 1 teaspoon hot chili-garlic sauce, such as Sriracha

- 3 cups cooked white or brown rice
- 4 medium carrots, grated
- 1 English cucumber, halved lengthwise and thinly sliced crosswise
- 1½ cups bean sprouts, roughly chopped
- 4 scallions (white and light green parts only), thinly sliced
- ½ cup chopped dry-roasted, salted peanuts

1. In a small bowl whisk the marinade ingredients. Place the steaks in a large, resealable plastic bag and pour in the marinade. Press the air out of the bag, seal tightly, and turn the bag several times to distribute the marinade. Refrigerate for 1 to 2 hours.

2. In a small bowl whisk the dressing ingredients.

3. Remove the steaks from the bag and discard the marinade. Allow the steaks to stand at room temperature for 15 to 30 minutes before grilling.

4. Prepare the grill for direct cooking over high heat (450° to 550°F).

5. Brush the cooking grates clean. Grill the steaks over ***direct high heat***, with the lid closed as much as possible, until cooked to your desired doneness, 4 to 6 minutes for medium rare, turning once or twice (if flare-ups occur, move the steaks temporarily over indirect heat). Transfer to a cutting board and let rest for 3 to 5 minutes.

6. Cut the steaks into thin slices. Put a scoop of rice in the center of each bowl or plate. Pile the vegetables in separate mounds around the rice, dividing the ingredients evenly. Whisk the dressing and pour it over the rice and vegetables (you may not need all of the dressing). Arrange the steak slices on top, and then sprinkle with the peanuts.

SERVES: 4

STEAK AND EGGS
WITH GREMOLATA

PREP TIME: 15 minutes
GRILLING TIME: 6 to 8 minutes

Gremolata
2 tablespoons finely chopped fresh Italian parsley leaves
½ teaspoon finely grated lemon zest
½ teaspoon finely grated garlic

4 New York strip steaks, each about 12 ounces and 1 inch thick, trimmed of excess fat
  Extra-virgin olive oil
  Kosher salt
  Ground black pepper

2 tablespoons unsalted butter
4 large eggs
4 slices bread, toasted (optional)
  Tabasco® sauce (optional)

Gremolata is an Italian condiment made of chopped parsley, grated lemon zest, and garlic. It can bring a spark of bright, fresh flavors to all sorts of grilled steaks.

1. In a small bowl mix the gremolata ingredients.

2. Lightly brush the steaks on both sides with oil and season with 1 teaspoon salt and ¾ teaspoon pepper. Allow the steaks to stand at room temperature for 15 to 30 minutes before grilling.

3. Prepare the grill for direct cooking over high heat (450° to 550°F).

4. Brush the cooking grates clean. Grill the steaks over ***direct high heat***, with the lid closed as much as possible, until cooked to your desired doneness, 6 to 8 minutes for medium rare, turning once or twice (if flare-ups occur, move the steaks temporarily over indirect heat). Remove from the grill and let rest for 3 to 5 minutes.

5. While the steaks rest, prepare the eggs. In a large nonstick skillet over medium heat, melt the butter. Crack the eggs into the skillet, being careful not to break the yolks. Season with salt and pepper. Cook until the whites are set, 3 to 5 minutes.

6. Cut the steaks into thin slices. Arrange a slice of toasted bread (if using) on each serving plate, place some sliced steak on the toast, lay the eggs over the meat, and sprinkle the gremolata on top. Add a bit of Tabasco, if desired. Serve warm.

SERVES: 4

FILET MIGNON STEAKS
WITH CRAB GUACAMOLE

PREP TIME: 25 minutes
GRILLING TIME: 16 to 20 minutes

Guacamole

- 1 large poblano chile pepper, 5 to 6 inches long
- 1 medium Hass avocado, diced
- 2 ounces cream cheese, softened
- 2 tablespoons fresh lime juice
- 4 ounces lump crabmeat
- 2 scallions (white and light green parts only), thinly sliced
- 1 tablespoon roughly chopped fresh cilantro leaves
- ½ teaspoon Tabasco® sauce
- ½ teaspoon kosher salt
- ⅛ teaspoon ground black pepper

- 4 filet mignon steaks, each about 8 ounces and 1½ inches thick
  Extra-virgin olive oil
  Kosher salt
  Ground black pepper

1. Prepare the grill for direct cooking over medium heat (350° to 450°F).

2. Brush the cooking grates clean. Grill the poblano chile over *direct medium heat*, with the lid closed as much as possible, until it is blackened and blistered in spots all over, 8 to 12 minutes, turning occasionally. Put the pepper in a bowl, cover with plastic wrap, and let steam for 10 minutes.

3. When the pepper is cool enough to handle, remove and discard the stem end, skin, and seeds. Drop the pepper into a food processor or blender. Add the avocado, cream cheese, and lime juice. Process to create a smooth guacamole. Pour the guacamole into a medium bowl, and fold in the crabmeat, scallions, and cilantro. Season with the Tabasco, salt, and pepper. Set aside at room temperature while you grill the steaks.

4. Lightly brush the steaks on both sides with oil and season evenly with salt and pepper. Allow the steaks to stand at room temperature for 15 to 30 minutes before grilling.

5. Increase the temperature of the grill to high heat (450° to 550°F). Grill the steaks over *direct high heat*, with the lid closed as much as possible, until cooked to your desired doneness, about 8 minutes for medium rare, turning once or twice (if flare-ups occur, move the steaks temporarily over indirect heat). Remove from the grill and let rest for 3 to 5 minutes. Serve the steaks warm with crab guacamole on top.

SERVES: 4

MEXICAN TENDERLOIN STRIPS
WITH AVOCADO, CHEESE, AND WARM TORTILLAS

PREP TIME: 20 minutes
MARINATING TIME: 1 to 2 hours
GRILLING TIME: 3 to 5 minutes

Marinade

- ¼ cup fresh lime juice
- ¼ cup extra-virgin olive oil
- 2 teaspoons kosher salt
- 1 teaspoon ground black pepper

- 4 filet mignon steaks, each 6 to 8 ounces and about 1½ inches thick

- 12 corn or flour tortillas (6 to 8 inches)
- 2 ripe Hass avocados, sliced
- 4 ounces queso fresco or feta cheese, crumbled
- ¼ cup fresh cilantro leaves
- 1 lime, quartered

1. In a large glass or stainless steel bowl, whisk the marinade ingredients.

2. Stand one steak on its side and, using a sharp chef's knife running perpendicular to the steak, make a cut about ½ inch deep toward the center of the steak. Then turn the knife 90 degrees and follow the shape of the steak all the way around the perimeter and then toward the center, unrolling the meat to obtain one long ½-inch-thick strip of meat. Repeat with the remaining filets. Place the meat in the bowl with the marinade and turn to coat evenly. Cover and refrigerate for 1 to 2 hours.

3. Prepare the grill for direct cooking over high heat (450° to 550°F).

4. Brush the cooking grates clean. Remove the strips of meat from the bowl, letting the excess marinade drip back into the bowl. Discard the marinade. Grill the steaks over ***direct high heat***, with the lid closed as much as possible, until the meat is cooked to your desired doneness, 2 to 4 minutes for medium rare, turning once or twice (if flare-ups occur, move the steaks temporarily over indirect heat). Transfer to a cutting board and let rest for about 2 minutes.

5. Warm the tortillas over ***direct high heat***, with the lid open, for about 30 seconds, turning once or twice.

6. Cut the strips of meat into thin slices. Arrange the meat, avocados, cheese, cilantro, limes, and tortillas on a large serving platter. Grab a tortilla, add some meat, and pile on your favorite toppings.

SERVES: 4

FILET MIGNON STEAKS
WITH ORANGE, HOISIN, AND GINGER SAUCE

PREP TIME: 15 minutes
GRILLING TIME: 6 to 8 minutes

Sauce
- 1 tablespoon minced fresh ginger
- 1 garlic clove, minced
- 1 teaspoon vegetable oil
- 1 tablespoon finely grated orange zest
- ⅓ cup fresh orange juice
- ¼ cup hoisin sauce

- 4 filet mignon steaks, each about 8 ounces and
     1 inch thick
     Vegetable oil
     Kosher salt
     Ground black pepper

1. In a small saucepan over low heat, gently cook the ginger and garlic in the oil until just fragrant, about 2 minutes. Whisk in the remaining sauce ingredients and simmer for 5 minutes. Remove from the heat.

2. Prepare the grill for direct cooking over high heat (450° to 550°F).

3. Lightly brush the steaks on both sides with oil and season evenly with salt and pepper. Allow the steaks to stand at room temperature for 15 to 30 minutes before grilling.

4. Brush the cooking grates clean. Grill the steaks over ***direct high heat***, with the lid closed as much as possible, until cooked to your desired doneness, 6 to 8 minutes for medium rare, turning once or twice (if flare-ups occur, move the steaks temporarily over indirect heat). Transfer to a serving platter and let rest for 3 to 5 minutes. Serve warm with the sauce. Serving suggestion: Pickled Cucumbers (for recipe, see page 123).

SERVES: 4

FILET MIGNON STEAKS
WITH GARLICKY SHRIMP

PREP TIME: 10 minutes
GRILLING TIME: 17 to 19 minutes

 4 filet mignon steaks, each about 8 ounces and
   1½ inches thick
   Extra-virgin olive oil
2½ teaspoons kosher salt, divided
 ½ teaspoon ground black pepper

 ½ cup (1 stick) unsalted butter
 2 large garlic cloves, coarsely chopped

12 extra-large shrimp (16/20 count), peeled and
   deveined, tails left on
   Finely grated zest of 1 lemon
 ¼ teaspoon crushed red pepper flakes

 2 tablespoons chopped fresh Italian parsley leaves

1. Lightly brush the steaks on both sides with oil and season evenly with 2 teaspoons of the salt and the pepper. Allow the steaks to stand at room temperature for 15 to 30 minutes before grilling.

2. Prepare the grill for direct cooking over medium heat (350° to 450°F).

3. In a small saucepan over medium heat, heat the butter and garlic until the butter melts and comes to a boil. Remove from the heat and let stand for 5 minutes.

4. Place the shrimp in a medium bowl and toss with 2 tablespoons of the garlic butter; reserve the remaining butter. Season the shrimp with the lemon zest, the remaining ½ teaspoon salt, and the red pepper flakes.

5. Brush the cooking grates clean. Grill the steaks over **_direct medium heat_**, with the lid closed as much as possible, until cooked to your desired doneness, 12 to 14 minutes for medium rare, turning once or twice (if flare-ups occur, move the steaks temporarily over indirect heat). Remove from the grill and let rest for 3 to 5 minutes.

6. Grill the shrimp over **_direct medium heat_**, with the lid closed as much as possible, until they are firm to the touch, lightly charred, and just turning opaque in the center, about 5 minutes, turning once.

7. Reheat the butter. Serve the steaks warm topped with shrimp, butter, and parsley.

SERVES: 4

PEPPER-CRUSTED FILET MIGNON STEAKS
WITH LEMON-PARSLEY BUTTER

PREP TIME: 15 minutes
GRILLING TIME: 12 to 14 minutes

Butter

- ¼ cup (½ stick) unsalted butter, softened
- 2 tablespoons minced fresh Italian parsley leaves
- ½ teaspoon finely grated lemon zest
- ¼ teaspoon kosher salt

Rub

- 1 tablespoon coarsely ground black peppercorns
- 1½ teaspoons kosher salt
- 1 teaspoon granulated garlic

- 4 filet mignon steaks, each about 8 ounces and 1½ inches thick
  Extra-virgin olive oil

1. In a small bowl combine the butter ingredients. Using the back of a fork, mash and stir until the ingredients are evenly distributed.

2. In a small bowl mix the rub ingredients.

3. Prepare the grill for direct cooking over medium heat (350° to 450°F).

4. Brush the steaks on both sides with oil and season evenly with the rub, pressing the spices into the meat. Allow the steaks to stand at room temperature for 15 to 30 minutes before grilling.

5. Brush the cooking grates clean. Grill the steaks over *direct medium heat*, with the lid closed as much as possible, until cooked to your desired doneness, 12 to 14 minutes for medium rare, turning once or twice (if flare-ups occur, move the steaks temporarily over indirect heat). Remove from the grill and let rest for 3 to 5 minutes. Serve the steaks warm with the butter smeared over the top. Serving suggestion: Melted Onions (for recipe, see page 116).

SERVES: 4

FILET MIGNON STEAKS
WITH BLACK OLIVE PESTO

PREP TIME: 15 minutes
GRILLING TIME: 6 to 8 minutes

Pesto
- 1 cup loosely packed fresh basil leaves
- 6 kalamata olives, pitted
- 1 tablespoon pine nuts
- 1 small garlic clove
- ¼ cup extra-virgin olive oil
- ¼ cup freshly grated Parmigiano-Reggiano® cheese

- 4 filet mignon steaks, each 6 to 8 ounces and about 1 inch thick
  Extra-virgin olive oil
- 1 teaspoon kosher salt
- ½ teaspoon ground black pepper

1. In a food processor finely chop the basil, olives, pine nuts, and garlic. Add the oil and cheese, and pulse briefly to incorporate the ingredients.

2. Brush the steaks on both sides with oil and season evenly with the salt and pepper. Allow the steaks to stand at room temperature for 15 to 30 minutes before grilling.

3. Prepare the grill for direct cooking over high heat (450° to 550°F).

4. Brush the cooking grates clean. Grill the steaks over ***direct high heat***, with the lid closed as much as possible, until cooked to your desired doneness, 6 to 8 minutes for medium rare, turning once or twice (if flare-ups occur, move the steaks temporarily over indirect heat). Remove from the grill and let rest for 3 to 5 minutes. Serve warm with the pesto spooned on top. Serving suggestion: Basic Grilled Asparagus (for recipe, see page 112).

SERVES: 4

FILET MIGNON CROSTINI
WITH BALSAMIC ONION JAM

Jam

- 2 tablespoons unsalted butter
- 2 tablespoons extra-virgin olive oil
- 2 large sweet yellow onions, about 12 ounces each, thinly sliced
- ½ teaspoon kosher salt
- ½ cup balsamic vinegar
- ½ cup packed light brown sugar
- ¼ cup dried currants or raisins

- 3 filet mignon steaks, each about 8 ounces and 1½ inches thick
- 1 tablespoon extra-virgin olive oil
- 1½ teaspoons kosher salt
- ¾ teaspoon ground black pepper

Crostini

- 1 baguette, cut into 25 slices, each ½ inch thick
  Extra-virgin olive oil
- 2 garlic cloves, peeled

- ⅓ cup sour cream
- 3 tablespoons prepared horseradish
- ¼ teaspoon kosher salt
- ½ teaspoon ground black pepper
- 1 bunch fresh chives (optional)

1. In a large skillet over medium-high heat, warm the butter and olive oil. Add the onions and salt. Cook until they become tender and have reduced in volume by half, about 10 minutes, stirring frequently to prevent burning. Stir in the vinegar, sugar, and currants. Reduce the heat to medium-low and cook until the onions become jam-like and most of the liquid has evaporated, about 35 minutes. Remove from the heat and let cool to room temperature. The jam will thicken as it cools. (The jam may be made up to 2 days ahead. Cover and refrigerate. Bring to room temperature before serving.)

For deep, rich flavors the onions should get as dark as this, but control the heat and keep stirring so they don't turn too black.

2. Prepare the grill for direct cooking over medium heat (350° to 450°F).

3. Lightly brush the steaks on both sides with the oil and season with the salt and pepper. Allow the steaks to stand at room temperature for 15 to 30 minutes before grilling.

52

4. Lightly brush one side of the baguette slices with oil and grill them over ***direct medium heat*** until toasted, 1 to 2 minutes (grill one side only). Allow to cool, and then rub the grilled sides lightly with the garlic.

5. In a small bowl combine the sour cream, horseradish, salt, and pepper. Cover and refrigerate until ready to use.

6. Grill the steaks over ***direct medium heat***, with the lid closed as much as possible, until cooked to your desired doneness, 12 to 14 minutes for medium rare, turning once or twice (if flare-ups occur, move the steaks temporarily over indirect heat). Remove from the grill and let rest for 3 to 5 minutes. Cut the steaks into ¼-inch slices.

7. Spread a layer of jam on each piece of toasted baguette (crostini). Place a slice of meat on the jam and top with a small dollop of the horseradish cream. Sprinkle with chopped fresh chives, if desired.

SERVES: 10 to 12

T-BONE STEAKS
WITH HORSERADISH-LEMON CREAM SAUCE

PREP TIME: 15 minutes
GRILLING TIME: 6 to 8 minutes

Rub

- 3 tablespoons finely chopped fresh rosemary leaves
- 6 large garlic cloves, minced
- 1 tablespoon kosher salt
- 1 teaspoon ground black pepper

- 4 T-bone steaks, each 12 to 16 ounces and about 1 inch thick, trimmed of excess fat
- 2 tablespoons extra-virgin olive oil

Sauce

- 1 cup sour cream
- 2 tablespoons plus 1 teaspoon prepared horseradish
- ¼ teaspoon finely grated lemon zest
- 2 tablespoons fresh lemon juice
- 2 tablespoons minced shallot
- 1 tablespoon finely chopped fresh Italian parsley leaves
- 2 teaspoons Worcestershire sauce
- ½ teaspoon kosher salt
- ½ teaspoon ground black pepper

1. In a small bowl combine the rub ingredients. Lightly brush the steaks on both sides with the oil and season evenly with the rub. Cover and allow the steaks to stand at room temperature for 15 to 30 minutes before grilling.

2. In a medium bowl combine the sauce ingredients and stir until well blended. The sauce should have the consistency of thick cream.

3. Prepare the grill for direct cooking over high heat (450° to 550°F).

4. Brush the cooking grates clean. Grill the steaks over **_direct high heat_**, with the lid closed as much as possible, until cooked to your desired doneness, 6 to 8 minutes for medium rare, turning once or twice (if flare-ups occur, move the steaks temporarily over indirect heat). Remove from the grill and let rest for 3 to 5 minutes. Serve warm with the sauce.

SERVES: 4 to 6

REALLY THICK T-BONES
WITH CREAMY WHITE BEANS

PREP TIME: 5 minutes, plus about 15 minutes
for the beans
GRILLING TIME: 10 to 14 minutes

Beans
- 1 cup finely chopped yellow onion
- ¼ cup extra-virgin olive oil
- 2 teaspoons minced garlic
- 2 cans (15 ounces each) cannellini beans, rinsed
- 1 cup tomato sauce
- ¼ cup heavy cream
- 1 tablespoon finely chopped fresh thyme leaves
  Kosher salt
  Ground black pepper

- 2 T-bone steaks, each about 1½ pounds and
  1½ inches thick, trimmed of excess fat
  Extra-virgin olive oil
- 1 tablespoon kosher salt
- 2 teaspoons ground black pepper

  Balsamic vinegar

1. In a large saucepan over medium heat, combine the onion and oil. Cook until the onion begins to brown, 8 to 10 minutes, stirring occasionally. Add the garlic and cook for 1 minute, stirring to prevent burning. Add the beans, tomato sauce, cream, and thyme. Mix well and bring the mixture to a simmer. Cook for a few minutes and then season with salt and pepper. Cover the saucepan and set aside.

2. Lightly brush the steaks on both sides with oil and season evenly with the salt and pepper. Allow the steaks to stand at room temperature for 15 to 30 minutes before grilling.

3. Prepare the grill for direct and indirect cooking over high heat (450° to 550°F).

4. Brush the cooking grates clean. Grill the steaks over **_direct high heat_**, with the lid closed as much as possible, until well marked on both sides, 6 to 8 minutes, turning once or twice. Move the steaks over **_indirect high heat_**, close the lid, and continue cooking to your desired doneness, 4 to 6 minutes for medium rare, turning once. Transfer to a cutting board and let rest for 3 to 5 minutes. Warm the beans, covered, over medium heat for a few minutes, stirring occasionally.

5. Cut the meat off the bones and then into ½-inch slices. Divide the beans equally in the center of each plate. Place several slices of steak on top of the beans. Drizzle any juices left on the cutting board over the steaks. Then add just a few drops of balsamic vinegar over each serving of steak and beans. Serve warm.

SERVES: 4

56

RANCHO T-BONES
WITH RED CHILE-HONEY GLAZE

PREP TIME: 10 minutes
GRILLING TIME: 8 to 10 minutes

Rub

- 2 teaspoons kosher salt
- 1 teaspoon ancho chile powder
- 1 teaspoon ground black pepper

- 4 T-bone steaks, each about 1 pound and 1¼ inches thick, trimmed of excess fat
  Extra-virgin olive oil

Glaze

- ¼ cup (½ stick) unsalted butter, softened
- 1 tablespoon honey
- 1 tablespoon fresh lime juice
- 2 teaspoons minced garlic
- ½ teaspoon ancho chile powder
- ½ teaspoon kosher salt
- ¼ teaspoon ground black pepper

1. In a small bowl mix the rub ingredients. Lightly brush the steaks on both sides with oil and season evenly with the rub. Allow the steaks to stand at room temperature for 15 to 30 minutes before grilling.

2. Prepare the grill for direct and indirect cooking over high heat (450° to 550°F).

3. In a small saucepan over medium heat, combine the glaze ingredients. Cook until the mixture reaches a simmer, 2 to 3 minutes. Remove the pan from the heat.

4. Brush the cooking grates clean. Grill the steaks over ***direct high heat***, with the lid closed as much as possible, for 6 minutes, turning once or twice. Move the steaks over ***indirect high heat***, brush them on both sides with some glaze, close the lid, and continue to cook to your desired doneness, 2 to 4 minutes for medium rare, turning and glazing once or twice. Remove the steaks from the grill and brush them on both sides with any remaining glaze. Let rest for 3 to 5 minutes. Serve warm.

SERVES: 4 to 6

ARGENTINEAN-STYLE T-BONE STEAKS
WITH SALSA CRIOLLA

PREP TIME: 15 minutes
GRILLING TIME: 6 to 8 minutes

Salsa

- 1 cup seeded, finely diced ripe tomato
- 1 cup finely diced green bell pepper
- ½ cup finely diced white onion, rinsed in a sieve under cold water
- 1 tablespoon red wine vinegar
- 1 tablespoon extra-virgin olive oil
- 1 teaspoon minced fresh oregano leaves
- 1 teaspoon kosher salt

- 4 T-bone steaks, each about 1 pound and 1 inch thick, trimmed of excess fat
  Extra-virgin olive oil
  Kosher salt
  Ground black pepper

NOTE
Raw onions can taste a little harsh in a salsa, but a good rinse under cold water will take the edge off.

1. In a medium glass or stainless steel bowl, combine the salsa ingredients. If desired, to fully incorporate the flavors, let the salsa sit at room temperature for up to an hour.

2. Lightly brush the steaks on both sides with oil and season evenly with salt and pepper. Allow the steaks to stand at room temperature for 15 to 30 minutes before grilling.

3. Prepare the grill for direct cooking over high heat (450° to 550°F).

4. Brush the cooking grates clean. Grill the steaks over *direct high heat*, with the lid closed as much as possible, until cooked to your desired doneness, 6 to 8 minutes for medium rare, turning once or twice (if flare-ups occur, move the steaks temporarily over indirect heat). Remove from the grill and let rest for 3 to 5 minutes. Serve warm with the salsa. Serving suggestion: Grilled Garlic Bread (for recipe, see page 125).

SERVES: 4 to 6

GINGER PORTERHOUSE STEAKS
WITH ROASTED SESAME SALT

PREP TIME: 20 minutes
GRILLING TIME: 6 to 8 minutes

3 tablespoons vegetable oil
2 tablespoons finely grated fresh ginger
2 teaspoons kosher salt
1½ teaspoons ground black pepper
2 porterhouse steaks, each about 1¼ pounds and 1 inch thick, trimmed of excess fat

Salt

3 tablespoons sesame seeds
1 teaspoon kosher salt
½ teaspoon ground black pepper

A blend of toasted sesame seeds with salt and pepper makes a wonderful condiment for seasoning the edge of individual steak slices.

1. In a small bowl mix the oil, ginger, salt, and pepper. Smear the mixture on both sides of each steak. Allow the steaks to stand at room temperature for 15 to 30 minutes before grilling.

2. Prepare the grill for direct cooking over high heat (450° to 550°F).

3. Heat a 10-inch skillet over medium heat. Add the salt ingredients. Cook until deep golden brown, 5 to 10 minutes, stirring occasionally with a wooden spoon to prevent burning. Divide the roasted salt evenly among four small dipping bowls.

4. Brush the cooking grates clean. Grill the steaks over **direct high heat**, with the lid closed as much as possible, until cooked to your desired doneness, 6 to 8 minutes for medium rare, turning once or twice (if flare-ups occur, move the steaks temporarily over indirect heat). Remove from the grill and let rest for 3 to 5 minutes. Serve warm with the salt. Guests are meant to dip an edge of each slice of steak in the salt.

SERVES: 4

PORTERHOUSE STEAKS
WITH HERBED VINAIGRETTE

PREP TIME: 15 minutes
GRILLING TIME: 8 to 10 minutes

Vinaigrette
- ¼ cup extra-virgin olive oil
- 3 tablespoons white wine vinegar
- 3 tablespoons chopped fresh herbs, such as basil, chives, Italian parsley, or your favorite combination
- 1 teaspoon minced shallot
- ½ teaspoon Dijon mustard
- ¼ teaspoon kosher salt
- ⅛ teaspoon ground black pepper

- 2 porterhouse steaks, each about 1¼ pounds and 1¼ inches thick, trimmed of excess fat
  Extra-virgin olive oil
- 1 teaspoon kosher salt
- ¾ teaspoon ground black pepper

1. In a small glass or stainless steel bowl, whisk the vinaigrette ingredients.

2. Lightly brush the steaks on both sides with oil and season with the salt and pepper. Allow the steaks to stand at room temperature for 15 to 30 minutes before grilling.

3. Prepare the grill for direct cooking over high heat (450° to 550°F).

4. Brush the cooking grates clean. Grill the steaks over **_direct high heat_**, with the lid closed as much as possible, until cooked to your desired doneness, 8 to 10 minutes for medium rare, turning once or twice (if flare-ups occur, move the steaks temporarily over indirect heat). Remove from the grill and let rest for 3 to 5 minutes.

5. Whisk the vinaigrette again. Cut the steaks into slices, place the slices on a platter, and spoon the vinaigrette over the top (you may not need all of the vinaigrette). Serve warm or at room temperature. Serving suggestion: Artichokes with Oregano and Salt (for recipe, see page 115).

SERVES: 4

PORTERHOUSE STEAKS
WITH SPICE CRUST AND GARLIC BUTTER

PREP TIME: 15 minutes
GRILLING TIME: 6 to 8 minutes
SPECIAL EQUIPMENT: spice mill

Rub

- 2 teaspoons black peppercorns
- 2 teaspoons mustard seed
- 2 teaspoons paprika
- 1 teaspoon granulated garlic
- 1 teaspoon kosher salt
- 1 teaspoon light brown sugar
- ¼ teaspoon cayenne chile powder

Butter

- 6 tablespoons (¾ stick) unsalted butter, cut into 6 pieces, softened
- 2 tablespoons Dijon mustard
- 1 large garlic clove, minced
- ¼ teaspoon ground black pepper

- 4 porterhouse steaks, each 12 to 16 ounces and about 1 inch thick, trimmed of excess fat
  Extra-virgin olive oil
  Sea salt

1. Crush the peppercorns and mustard seed in a spice mill. Pour into a small bowl and add the remaining rub ingredients. Mix thoroughly.

2. In a small bowl combine the butter ingredients along with ½ teaspoon of the rub. Using the back of a fork, mash the ingredients together, distributing them evenly. Cover and refrigerate the butter, if making ahead. Otherwise, the butter can remain at room temperature while you prepare and grill the steaks.

3. Lightly brush the steaks on both sides with oil and season evenly with the rub, pressing the spices into the meat. Allow the steaks to stand at room temperature for 15 to 30 minutes before grilling.

4. Prepare the grill for direct cooking over high heat (450° to 550°F).

5. Brush the cooking grates clean. Grill the steaks over ***direct high heat***, with the lid closed as much as possible, until cooked to your desired doneness, 6 to 8 minutes for medium rare, turning once or twice (if flare-ups occur, move the steaks temporarily over indirect heat). Remove from the grill and let rest for 3 to 5 minutes.

6. Season the steaks with salt and serve with a spoonful of butter smeared over the top.

SERVES: 4 to 6

PORTERHOUSE STEAKS
WITH BÉARNAISE SAUCE

PREP TIME: 15 minutes
GRILLING TIME: 6 to 8 minutes

2 porterhouse steaks, each about 1¼ pounds and 1 inch thick, trimmed of excess fat
Extra-virgin olive oil
Kosher salt
Ground black pepper

Sauce

3 tablespoons dry white wine
3 tablespoons white wine vinegar
2 tablespoons minced shallot
3 egg yolks (see note below)
¾ cup (1½ sticks) unsalted butter, melted
¼ teaspoon kosher salt
⅛ teaspoon ground black pepper
2 tablespoons finely chopped fresh tarragon leaves

NOTE!

Using raw egg yolks to make béarnaise sauce could cause salmonella poisoning. To avoid that risk, use yolks from pasteurized eggs.

1. Lightly brush the steaks on both sides with oil and season evenly with salt and pepper. Allow the steaks to stand at room temperature for 15 to 30 minutes before grilling.

2. Prepare the grill for direct cooking over high heat (450° to 550°F).

3. In a small saucepan over high heat, bring the wine, vinegar, and shallot to a boil. Cook until the liquid is reduced to about 2 tablespoons, about 2 minutes. Strain through a sieve into a small bowl; reserve the vinegar mixture and discard the shallot.

4. Place the yolks in a blender. With the machine running on high, drizzle in the vinegar mixture through the hole in the blender lid. Pouring in a slow stream, gradually add the melted butter. The sauce should be thick and have the consistency of mayonnaise. Season with the salt and pepper. Transfer the sauce to a small heat-proof bowl. Stir in the tarragon. Place the bowl over a water bath of very hot, but not simmering, water to keep the sauce warm while grilling the steaks.

5. Brush the cooking grates clean. Grill the steaks over ***direct high heat***, with the lid closed as much as possible, until cooked to your desired doneness, 6 to 8 minutes for medium rare, turning once or twice (if flare-ups occur, move the steaks temporarily over indirect heat). Remove from the grill and let rest for 3 to 5 minutes. Cut the steaks into slices, and arrange the slices on serving plates. Serve warm with the sauce.

SERVES: 4

PACIFIC RIM FLANK STEAK
WITH VEGETABLE MEDLEY

PREP TIME: 30 minutes
MARINATING TIME: 3 to 4 hours
GRILLING TIME: 11 to 15 minutes
SPECIAL EQUIPMENT: perforated grill pan

Marinade

- ½ cup soy sauce
- 2 tablespoons oyster sauce
- 2 tablespoons rice vinegar
- 2 tablespoons toasted sesame oil
- 2 tablespoons minced fresh ginger
- ¼ teaspoon crushed red pepper flakes

- 1 flank steak, 1½ to 2 pounds and about ¾ inch thick

- 1 large red bell pepper, cut into ¼-inch-wide strips
- 1 large zucchini, cut into ¼-inch-thick half-moons
- 1 medium red onion, cut into ¼-inch-thick half-moons
- 1 medium Japanese eggplant, cut into ¼-inch-thick slices
  Vegetable oil

  Kosher salt
  Ground black pepper
  Toasted sesame oil

1. In a medium bowl whisk the marinade ingredients. Put 2 tablespoons of the marinade in a large bowl.

2. Put the steak in a 13x9-inch glass dish and pour in the marinade. Turn to coat both sides. Cover and refrigerate for 3 to 4 hours, turning occasionally. Allow the steak to stand at room temperature for 15 to 30 minutes before grilling.

3. Prepare the grill for direct cooking over high heat (450° to 550°F).

4. Put the bell pepper, zucchini, onion, and eggplant in the large bowl with the reserved marinade. Add just enough vegetable oil to coat them lightly.

5. Brush the cooking grates clean. Remove the steak from the marinade, letting most of the marinade drip back into the dish. Discard the marinade. Grill the steak over *direct high heat*, with the lid closed as much as possible, until cooked to your desired doneness, 6 to 8 minutes for medium rare, turning once or twice (if flare-ups occur, move the steak temporarily over indirect heat). Transfer to a cutting board and let rest while you grill the vegetables.

6. Preheat a grill pan over *direct high heat* for about 10 minutes. Spread the vegetables on the grill pan in a single layer, close the lid, and grill until the vegetables are crisp-tender, 5 to 7 minutes, stirring occasionally. Transfer to a large platter, season with salt and pepper, and add a few drops of sesame oil. Cut the steak across the grain into thin slices and serve warm with the vegetables.

SERVES: 4 to 6

STEAK AND TOMATO WRAPS
WITH AVOCADO SAUCE

PREP TIME: 30 minutes
GRILLING TIME: 8 to 12 minutes

Sauce
- 1 medium Hass avocado, diced
- ½ cup finely diced English cucumber
- ¼ cup sour cream
- ¼ cup thinly sliced scallions (white and light green parts only)
- ¼ cup roughly chopped fresh dill
- 2 tablespoons lime juice
- ¼ teaspoon Tabasco® sauce
- ¼ teaspoon kosher salt

Rub
- 2 teaspoons granulated garlic
- 2 teaspoons dried oregano
- 1 teaspoon kosher salt
- ¼ teaspoon ground black pepper

- 1 flank steak, about 1½ pounds and ¾ inch thick
- 2 large red onions, cut crosswise into ½-inch slices
  Extra-virgin olive oil
- 4 large lettuce leaves
- 4 flour tortillas (10 inches)
- 4 plum tomatoes, roughly chopped

1. In a food processor or blender, puree the sauce ingredients until smooth. Pour the sauce into a small bowl, cover, and refrigerate until ready to use. (The sauce may be made up to 1 day ahead.)

2. In a small bowl combine the rub ingredients. Lightly brush the steak and onions on both sides with oil and season evenly with the rub. Allow the steak to stand at room temperature for 15 to 30 minutes before grilling.

3. Prepare the grill for direct cooking over medium heat (350° to 450°F).

4. Brush the cooking grates clean. Grill the steak and onions over **direct medium heat**, with the lid closed as much as possible, until the steak is cooked to your desired doneness and the onions are tender, turning once or twice (if flare-ups occur, move the steak temporarily over indirect heat). The steak will take 8 to 10 minutes for medium-rare doneness, and the onions will take 8 to 12 minutes. Remove from the grill and let the steak rest for 3 to 5 minutes. While the steak rests, warm the tortillas over **direct medium heat** for 30 seconds to 1 minute, turning once or twice.

5. Cut the steak in half lengthwise, and then cut each half across the grain into thin slices. Cut the slices into bite-sized pieces. Roughly chop the onions.

6. Place a lettuce leaf in the center of each tortilla and top with steak, onions, tomatoes, and a dollop of avocado sauce. Roll up and serve warm.

SERVES: 4

TAGLIATA OF FLANK STEAK
WITH ARUGULA AND SHAVED PARMESAN

PREP TIME: 15 minutes
GRILLING TIME: 6 to 8 minutes

1 flank steak, 1½ to 2 pounds and about
   ¾ inch thick
   Extra-virgin olive oil
   Kosher salt
   Ground black pepper

⅓ cup balsamic vinegar
½ teaspoon granulated sugar

6 cups loosely packed baby arugula
1 cup loosely packed shaved Parmigiano-
   Reggiano® cheese

1. Lightly brush the steak on both sides with oil and season evenly with salt and pepper. Allow the steak to stand at room temperature for 15 to 30 minutes before grilling.

2. Prepare the grill for direct cooking over high heat (450° to 550°F).

3. In a small saucepan over medium-high heat, combine the vinegar and sugar. Allow the mixture to reduce by half, 6 to 8 minutes, stirring occasionally. Remove from the heat and let cool.

4. Brush the cooking grates clean. Grill the steak over **direct high heat**, with the lid closed as much as possible, until cooked to your desired doneness, 6 to 8 minutes for medium rare, turning once or twice (if flare-ups occur, move the steak temporarily over indirect heat). Transfer to a cutting board and let rest for 3 to 5 minutes.

5. Cut the steak in half lengthwise and then cut each half across the grain into thin slices; divide evenly on serving plates. Pour any juices remaining on the cutting board over the steak, and pile the arugula on top. Drizzle each serving of arugula with oil and the balsamic reduction, season with salt and pepper, and top with the cheese.

SERVES: 4 to 6

FLANK STEAK SATAY
WITH PEANUT SAUCE

PREP TIME: 30 minutes
MARINATING TIME: 30 minutes to 1 hour
GRILLING TIME: 4 to 6 minutes
SPECIAL EQUIPMENT: metal or bamboo skewers
(if using bamboo, soak in water for at least
30 minutes)

Marinade
- 2 tablespoons vegetable oil
- 1 tablespoon finely chopped fresh ginger
- 1 tablespoon fresh lime juice
- 1 tablespoon soy sauce
- 1 tablespoon finely chopped garlic
- 2 teaspoons ground coriander

- 1 flank steak, about 1½ pounds and ¾ inch thick

Sauce
- 1 cup unsweetened coconut milk, stirred
- ⅓ cup creamy peanut butter
- 1 teaspoon finely grated lime zest
- 3 tablespoons fresh lime juice
- 1 tablespoon soy sauce
- 1 tablespoon brown sugar
- 1 teaspoon hot chili-garlic sauce, such as Sriracha
- ½ teaspoon grated fresh ginger

1. In a medium glass or stainless steel bowl, mix the marinade ingredients.

2. Cut the steak in half lengthwise and then cut each half across the grain into slices about ½ inch thick. Add the slices to the marinade and toss to coat. Cover and marinate at room temperature for 30 minutes or in the refrigerator for 1 hour, turning occasionally. (If refrigerated, allow the steak to stand at room temperature for 15 to 30 minutes before grilling.)

3. In a heavy-bottomed saucepan over medium heat, combine the sauce ingredients. Cook, but do not simmer, just until the sauce is smooth and slightly thickened, 2 to 3 minutes, whisking constantly (the sauce will thicken as it cools). Remove from the heat.

4. Prepare the grill for direct cooking over high heat (450° to 550°F).

5. Thread the slices of steak onto skewers. Discard the marinade.

6. Brush the cooking grates clean. Grill the skewers over ***direct high heat***, with the lid closed as much as possible, until cooked to your desired doneness, 4 to 6 minutes for medium rare, turning once or twice (if flare-ups occur, move the skewers temporarily over indirect heat). Remove the steak skewers from the grill and serve warm with the sauce.

SERVES: 4

FLANK STEAK GYROS
WITH FRESH CUCUMBER SALAD

PREP TIME: 45 minutes
MARINATING TIME: 2 to 4 hours
GRILLING TIME: 8 to 10 minutes

Marinade
- ½ cup extra-virgin olive oil
- ¼ cup fresh lemon juice
- ¼ cup roughly chopped fresh oregano leaves
- 1 tablespoon minced garlic
- 2 teaspoons coarsely ground black pepper
- ½ teaspoon kosher salt

- 1 flank steak, 1½ to 2 pounds and about ¾ inch thick

Salad
- 2 cups coarsely shredded romaine lettuce
- 25 kalamata olives, pitted
- 1 cup peeled, finely diced English cucumber
- 1 cup finely diced ripe tomato
- ½ cup finely diced red onion

Sauce
- 1 cup Greek yogurt
- 3 tablespoons finely chopped fresh mint leaves
- ½ teaspoon kosher salt
- ¼ teaspoon ground black pepper

- 4 pita bread pockets, cut in half

1. In a medium bowl whisk the marinade ingredients. Set aside ¼ cup of the marinade to dress the salad.

2. Put the steak in a 13x9-inch glass dish and pour in the marinade. Turn to coat both sides. Cover and refrigerate for 2 to 4 hours, turning occasionally. Allow the steak to stand at room temperature for 15 to 30 minutes before grilling.

3. In a medium bowl combine the salad ingredients and set aside until ready to serve.

4. Prepare the grill for direct cooking over medium heat (350° to 450°F).

5. Brush the cooking grates clean. Remove the steak from the marinade, letting the excess liquid drip back into the dish. Discard the marinade. Grill the steak over ***direct medium heat***, with the lid closed as much as possible, until cooked to your desired doneness, 8 to 10 minutes for medium rare, turning once or twice (if flare-ups occur, move the steak temporarily over indirect heat). Remove from the grill and let rest for 3 to 5 minutes.

6. Cut the steak in half lengthwise and then across the grain into thin slices. Cut the slices into bite-sized pieces.

7. In a small bowl whisk the sauce ingredients.

8. Dress the salad with the reserved marinade and toss to coat. Fill each pita half with steak, salad, and then top with a spoonful of sauce. Serve warm.

SERVES: 4 to 6

STEAK TACOS
WITH GRILLED TOMATILLO SALSA

PREP TIME: 20 minutes
GRILLING TIME: 14 to 18 minutes

Salsa
- 1 small white onion, quartered
- ½ pound tomatillos, husks removed and rinsed
  Extra-virgin olive oil
- 1 serrano chile pepper
- 1 Hass avocado, diced
  Kosher salt
  Ground black pepper

Rub
- 1 teaspoon prepared chili powder
- 1 teaspoon kosher salt
- ½ teaspoon ground black pepper

- 1 flank steak, 1½ to 2 pounds and about ¾ inch thick

- 12 corn tortillas (6 to 8 inches)
- 1 cup cherry tomatoes, cut into quarters
- 1 cup fresh cilantro leaves

1. Prepare the grill for direct cooking over high heat (450° to 550°F).

2. Lightly brush the onion and tomatillos with oil. Brush the cooking grates clean. Grill the onion, tomatillos, and chile over *direct high heat*, with the lid closed as much as possible, until charred on all sides and softened, 8 to 10 minutes. When cool enough to handle, remove and discard the stem and seeds from the chile. Place the onion, tomatillos, chile, and avocado in a food processor or blender. Pulse until you have a thick pureed salsa. Transfer to a bowl and season with salt and pepper.

3. In a small bowl combine the rub ingredients. Lightly brush the steak on both sides with oil and season evenly with the rub. Allow the steak to stand at room temperature for 15 to 30 minutes before grilling.

4. Grill the steak over *direct high heat*, with the lid closed as much as possible, until cooked to your desired doneness, 6 to 8 minutes for medium rare, turning once or twice (if flare-ups occur, move the steak temporarily over indirect heat). Transfer to a cutting board and let rest for 3 to 5 minutes. Cut the steak across the grain into thin slices.

5. Warm the tortillas over *direct high heat*, with the lid open, for about 30 seconds, turning once or twice. Serve the tacos family style, with the steak, salsa, tortillas, tomatoes, and cilantro in separate bowls.

SERVES: 4 to 6

MARINATED FLANK STEAK
WITH CREOLE FLAVORS

PREP TIME: 10 minutes
MARINATING TIME: 30 minutes
GRILLING TIME: 8 to 10 minutes

Marinade

- 3 tablespoons Creole mustard
- 3 tablespoons extra-virgin olive oil
- 3 tablespoons red wine vinegar
- 2 teaspoons Worcestershire sauce
- 2 teaspoons minced garlic
- 1 teaspoon dried thyme
- ½ teaspoon kosher salt
- ½ teaspoon ground black pepper

- 1 flank steak, 1½ to 2 pounds and about ¾ inch thick

1. In a small bowl whisk the marinade ingredients. Place the steak in a large, resealable plastic bag and pour in the marinade. Press the air out of the bag and seal tightly. Turn the bag to distribute the marinade, place the bag on a plate, and marinate at room temperature for 30 minutes, turning once or twice.

2. Prepare the grill for direct cooking over medium heat (350° to 450°F).

3. Brush the cooking grates clean. Remove the steak from the bag and wipe off most of the marinade clinging to the steak. Discard the marinade. Grill the steak over ***direct medium heat***, with the lid closed as much as possible, until cooked to your desired doneness, 8 to 10 minutes for medium rare, turning once or twice (if flare-ups occur, move the steak temporarily over indirect heat). Remove from the grill and let rest for 3 to 5 minutes.

4. Cut the steak across the grain into thin slices and serve warm. Serving suggestion: Cajun Corn with Louisiana Butter (for recipe, see page 120).

SERVES: 4 to 6

FLANK STEAK
MARINATED IN TERIYAKI AND BOURBON

PREP TIME: 10 minutes
MARINATING TIME: 2 to 3 hours
GRILLING TIME: 8 to 10 minutes

Marinade
⅓ cup teriyaki sauce
¼ cup bourbon or whiskey
¼ cup extra-virgin olive oil
2 tablespoons dark brown sugar
1 tablespoon stone-ground mustard
2 teaspoons minced garlic
1 teaspoon crushed red pepper flakes
½ teaspoon kosher salt

1 flank steak, 1½ to 2 pounds and about
¾ inch thick

1. In a small bowl whisk the marinade ingredients. Place the steak in a 13x9-inch glass dish and pour in the marinade. Turn the steak to coat both sides. Cover and refrigerate for 2 to 3 hours, turning the steak once or twice.

2. Allow the steak to stand at room temperature for 15 to 30 minutes before grilling.

3. Prepare the grill for direct cooking over medium heat (350° to 450°F).

4. Brush the cooking grates clean. Lift the steak from the marinade and let the excess marinade drip back into the dish. Discard the marinade. Grill the steak over *direct medium heat*, with the lid closed as much as possible, until cooked to your desired doneness, 8 to 10 minutes for medium rare, turning once or twice (if flare-ups occur, move the steak temporarily over indirect heat). Transfer to a cutting board and let rest for 3 to 5 minutes.

5. Cut the steak across the grain into thin slices. Serve warm. Serving suggestion: Glazed Sweet Potatoes (for recipe, see page 118).

SERVES: 4 to 6

ITALIAN BEEF SANDWICHES
WITH PICKLED VEGETABLES

PREP TIME: 25 minutes
GRILLING TIME: 9 to 11 minutes

Rub

- 1 teaspoon dried oregano
- 1 teaspoon dried thyme
- ¾ teaspoon kosher salt
- ½ teaspoon ground black pepper
- ¼ teaspoon granulated garlic

- 1 flank steak, 1½ to 2 pounds and about ¾ inch thick
  Extra-virgin olive oil

- 2 cups low-sodium beef broth
- ½ cup dry red wine
- 1 garlic clove, thinly sliced
  Kosher salt
  Ground black pepper

- 6 Italian rolls, each about 6 inches long, split
- 1 jar (16 ounces) pickled Italian vegetables (*giardiniera*), drained and thinly sliced

1. In a small bowl mix the rub ingredients. Lightly brush the steak on both sides with oil and season evenly with the rub. Allow the steak to stand at room temperature for 15 to 30 minutes before grilling.

2. Prepare the grill for direct cooking over medium heat (350° to 450°F).

3. In a medium saucepan over high heat, bring the broth, wine, and garlic to a simmer. Reduce the heat to low and cook for 15 minutes. Season with salt and pepper. Keep warm.

4. Brush the cooking grates clean. Grill the steak over **direct medium heat**, with the lid closed as much as possible, until cooked to your desired doneness, 8 to 10 minutes for medium rare, turning once or twice (if flare-ups occur, move the steak temporarily over indirect heat). Transfer to a cutting board and let rest for 3 to 5 minutes.

5. While the steak rests, toast the rolls, cut sides down, over **direct medium heat**, for 30 seconds to 1 minute.

6. Pour the broth into six small serving bowls or ramekins. Cut the steak in half lengthwise and then cut across the grain into thin slices. Pile the bottom of each toasted roll with steak and some pickled vegetables. Cut each sandwich in half crosswise. Serve warm with the broth for dipping.

SERVES: 6

76

SKIRT STEAK FAJITAS
WITH JALAPEÑO SALSA

PREP TIME: 30 minutes
MARINATING TIME: 30 minutes
GRILLING TIME: 12 to 16 minutes

Marinade
¼ cup fresh lime juice
2 tablespoons vegetable oil
2 teaspoons light brown sugar
1 teaspoon minced garlic
1 teaspoon ground cumin
1 teaspoon kosher salt

2 pounds skirt steak, ½ to ¾ inch thick, trimmed of excess surface fat, cut into foot-long pieces

Salsa
1½ cups coarsely chopped ripe tomatoes
2 large Hass avocados, diced
¼ cup roughly chopped fresh cilantro leaves
3 tablespoons finely chopped scallions (white part only)
1–2 jalapeño chile peppers, minced, with seeds
1 tablespoon fresh lime juice
¼ teaspoon Tabasco® sauce
Kosher salt
Ground black pepper

2 large yellow onions, cut crosswise into ½-inch slices
2 large red bell peppers, cut into flat slices, ribs and seeds removed
Vegetable oil

8 flour tortillas (10 inches)

1. In a small bowl whisk the marinade ingredients. Place the steaks in a large, resealable plastic bag and pour in the marinade. Press the air out of the bag and seal tightly. Turn the bag to distribute the marinade. Marinate at room temperature for 30 minutes, turning the bag occasionally.

2. Prepare the grill for direct cooking over high heat (450° to 550°F).

3. In a medium bowl combine the salsa ingredients, and season with salt and pepper.

4. Brush the cooking grates clean. Brush the onion and pepper slices with oil and grill them over ***direct high heat***, with the lid closed as much as possible, until they are lightly charred and softened, 6 to 8 minutes, turning once or twice. Remove from the grill and allow to cool. Roughly chop the onions, and slice the peppers into ¼-inch strips.

5. Remove the steaks from the bag, allowing most of the marinade to drip back into the bag. Discard the marinade. Grill the steaks over ***direct high heat***, with the lid closed as much as possible, until cooked to your desired doneness, 4 to 6 minutes for medium rare, turning once or twice (if flare-ups occur, move the steaks temporarily over indirect heat). Remove from the grill and let rest for 3 to 5 minutes.

6. Wrap the tortillas in foil and warm them over ***direct high heat***, about 2 minutes, turning once. Cut the steaks across the grain into thin slices. Serve with the onions, peppers, tortillas, and salsa.

SERVES: 4 to 6

BALSAMIC-MARINATED SKIRT STEAKS

WITH GRILLED SMASHED POTATOES AND OLIVE AIOLI

PREP TIME: 15 minutes, plus about 30 minutes for the potatoes
MARINATING TIME: 30 minutes to 2 hours
GRILLING TIME: 4 to 6 minutes

Marinade

⅓ cup balsamic vinegar
¼ cup extra-virgin olive oil
¼ cup chopped fresh rosemary leaves

2 pounds skirt steak, ½ to ¾ inch thick, trimmed of excess surface fat, cut into foot-long pieces

Potatoes

Kosher salt
1 pound red or white new potatoes, each about the size of a golf ball
2 tablespoons extra-virgin olive oil
Ground black pepper

Aioli

½ cup good-quality mayonnaise
1 tablespoon black olive tapenade
1 teaspoon fresh lemon juice
1 teaspoon minced garlic

1. In a large glass or stainless steel bowl, whisk the marinade ingredients. Place the steaks in the bowl, turn, and rub the marinade in with your fingertips to coat all sides of the meat. Cover and refrigerate for at least 30 minutes or up to 2 hours.

2. Fill a large pot with water and add enough salt so it tastes like seawater (⅓ cup salt to 8 cups water). Add the potatoes and bring to a boil. Cook until tender, 20 to 30 minutes, depending on the size of the potatoes. Drain, and let the potatoes rest until they are cool enough to handle. Use the bottom of a small saucepan and gently press on each potato to smash it to an even thickness, about ¾ inch thick. Brush both sides with oil and season with salt and pepper.

Boil the potatoes first, smash them under a pan like this, and then grill them along with the steaks until brown and crispy.

3. In a medium bowl mix the aioli ingredients. Cover and refrigerate until serving.

4. Prepare the grill for direct cooking over high heat (450° to 550°F).

5. Remove the steaks from the bowl and discard the marinade. Pat the steaks dry with paper towels and season evenly with salt and pepper. Brush the cooking grates clean. Grill the steaks over **direct high heat**, with the lid closed as much as possible, until cooked to your desired doneness, 4 to 6 minutes for medium rare, turning once or twice (if flare-ups occur, move the steaks temporarily over indirect heat). Grill the potatoes while you grill the steaks, and cook them until they begin to brown and crisp, about 5 minutes, turning once. Let the steaks rest for 3 to 5 minutes. Cut the steaks across the grain into ¼-inch-thick slices, and serve with the potatoes and the aioli.

SERVES: 4

STEAK AND SPINACH SALAD
WITH SESAME-GINGER DRESSING

PREP TIME: 30 minutes
GRILLING TIME: 12 to 16 minutes

Dressing

- ¼ cup canola oil
- 2 tablespoons fresh lime juice
- 1 tablespoon soy sauce
- 2 teaspoons light brown sugar
- 2 teaspoons toasted sesame oil
- ½ teaspoon grated fresh ginger
- ¼ teaspoon crushed red pepper flakes

- 1¼ pounds skirt steak, ½ to ¾ inch thick, trimmed of excess surface fat, cut into foot-long pieces
- 2 medium red onions, cut crosswise into ⅓-inch slices
- 4 cups loosely packed baby spinach leaves, about 4 ounces
- ½ cup salted, dry-roasted peanuts
- ½ cup roughly chopped fresh mint leaves
  Kosher salt
  Ground black pepper

1. In a medium bowl whisk the dressing ingredients until smooth.

2. Place the steaks on a sheet pan. Coat them on both sides with about one-third of the dressing. On another sheet pan coat the onion slices with another one-third of the dressing. Allow the steaks and onions to stand at room temperature for 15 to 30 minutes before grilling.

3. Prepare the grill for direct cooking over medium heat (350° to 450°F).

4. Brush the cooking grates clean. Grill the onions over ***direct medium heat***, with the lid closed as much as possible, until lightly charred and tender, 8 to 10 minutes, turning once or twice. Remove the onions from the grill and roughly chop them. Increase the temperature of the grill to high heat (450° to 550°F).

5. Grill the steaks over ***direct high heat***, with the lid closed as much as possible, until cooked to your desired doneness, 4 to 6 minutes for medium rare, turning once or twice (if flare-ups occur, move the steaks temporarily over indirect heat). Remove from the grill and let rest for 3 to 5 minutes. Cut the steaks across the grain into thin slices.

6. Put the warm steak slices in a large bowl. Add the onions, spinach, peanuts, and mint. Whisk the remaining dressing and use some of it to coat the salad ingredients lightly (you may not need all of the dressing). Season with salt and pepper. Serve right away.

SERVES: 4

ROSEMARY-GARLIC SKIRT STEAKS
WITH SHIITAKE MUSHROOMS

PREP TIME: 20 minutes
GRILLING TIME: 4 to 6 minutes
SPECIAL EQUIPMENT: perforated grill pan

Marinade
- ½ cup extra-virgin olive oil
- 2 tablespoons red wine vinegar
- 2 tablespoons chopped fresh rosemary leaves
- 1 tablespoon minced garlic
- 1 tablespoon kosher salt
- 1 teaspoon ground black pepper

- 1 pound shiitake mushrooms, cleaned and stems removed
- 1½ pounds skirt steak, ½ to ¾ inch thick, trimmed of excess surface fat, cut into foot-long pieces
- 1 tablespoon finely chopped fresh thyme or Italian parsley leaves

1. In a large glass or stainless steel bowl, whisk the marinade ingredients. Put the mushrooms in another large glass or stainless steel bowl, whisk the marinade again, and pour about half of it over the mushrooms. Gently toss the mushrooms to coat them evenly. Add the steaks to the remaining marinade and turn to coat evenly. Allow the steaks and mushrooms to stand at room temperature for 15 to 30 minutes before grilling.

2. Prepare the grill for direct cooking over high heat (450° to 550°F). Brush the cooking grates clean. Place a grill pan on one side of the cooking grate and let it preheat for at least 10 minutes.

3. Lift the steaks from the marinade and let the excess drip back into the bowl. Discard the marinade. Grill the steaks over *direct high heat*, with the lid closed as much as possible, until cooked to your desired doneness, 4 to 6 minutes for medium rare, turning once or twice (if flare-ups occur, move the steaks temporarily over indirect heat). At the same time, grill the mushrooms on the grill pan, carefully lifting the mushrooms from the marinade and spreading them in a single layer. Cook until darkened in spots and tender throughout, 3 to 4 minutes, turning occasionally. Transfer the mushrooms to a bowl as they are done. Remove the steaks from the grill and let rest for 3 to 5 minutes.

4. Cut the steaks across the grain into ¼-inch-thick slices and arrange them on a platter or individual plates. Surround the meat with the mushrooms. Sprinkle the fresh herbs over the top. Serve warm.

SERVES: 4

SKIRT STEAKS
WITH POBLANO AND CHERRY TOMATO SALSA

PREP TIME: 20 minutes
MARINATING TIME: 1 hour
GRILLING TIME: 14 to 18 minutes

Marinade

- 3 tablespoons extra-virgin olive oil
- 2 tablespoons balsamic vinegar
- 1 tablespoon minced garlic
- 1½ teaspoons smoked paprika
- 1 teaspoon kosher salt
- ½ teaspoon ground black pepper

- 2 pounds skirt steak, ½ to ¾ inch thick, trimmed of excess surface fat, cut into foot-long pieces

Salsa

- 1 medium red onion, cut crosswise into ½-inch slices
  Extra-virgin olive oil
- 3 medium poblano chile peppers
- 1 medium yellow bell pepper
- 1 pound small cherry tomatoes, stemmed, quartered
- ½ teaspoon balsamic vinegar
- ⅛ teaspoon kosher salt

1. In a small bowl whisk the marinade ingredients. Place the steaks in a large, resealable plastic bag and pour in the marinade. Press the air out of the bag and seal tightly. Turn the bag to distribute the marinade, place in a bowl, and refrigerate for 1 hour.

2. Prepare the grill for direct cooking over high heat (450° to 550°F).

3. Brush the cooking grates clean. Brush the onion slices with oil, and grill them, along with the poblanos and bell pepper, over *direct high heat*, with the lid closed as much as possible, until the onions are tender and the peppers are blackened and blistered all over, 8 to 12 minutes, turning occasionally. Place the peppers in a large bowl and cover with plastic wrap to trap the steam. Set aside for at least 10 minutes.

4. Remove the steaks from the bag and discard the marinade. Allow the steaks to stand at room temperature for 15 to 30 minutes before grilling.

5. Remove the skin, stems, and seeds from the peppers. Cut the peppers and onion into ½-inch pieces and place in a large bowl. Add the tomatoes, vinegar, and salt.

6. Grill the steaks over *direct high heat*, with the lid closed as much as possible, until cooked to your desired doneness, 4 to 6 minutes for medium rare, turning once or twice (if flare-ups occur, move the steaks temporarily over indirect heat). Remove from the grill and let rest for 3 to 5 minutes. Cut the steaks across the grain and serve warm with the salsa.

SERVES: 4 to 6

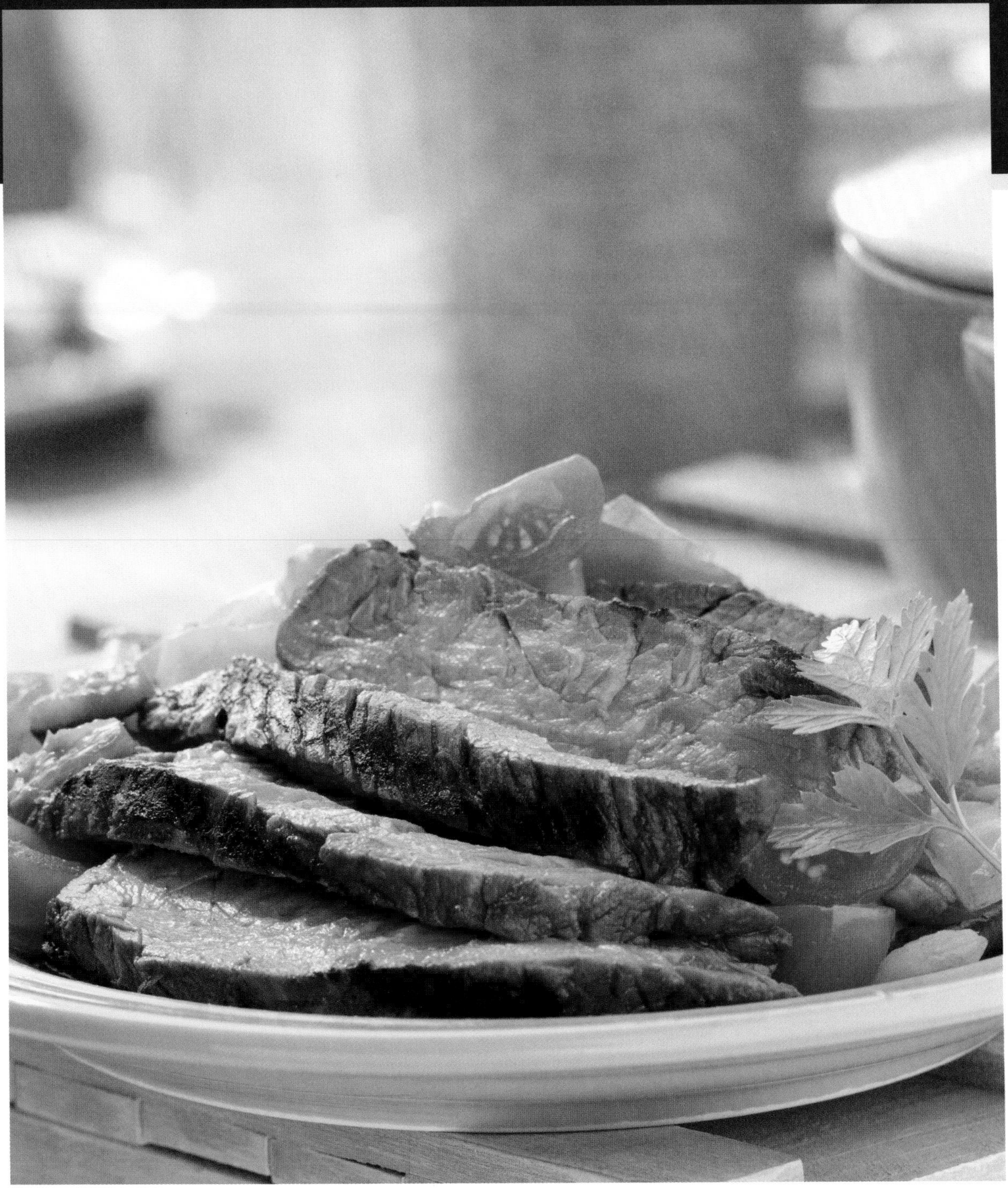

TOP SIRLOIN STEAK
WITH SANTA FE SPICE RUB

PREP TIME: 10 minutes
GRILLING TIME: 10 to 12 minutes

Rub

1½ teaspoons kosher salt
 1 teaspoon ground black pepper
 1 teaspoon ground cumin
 1 teaspoon light brown sugar
 ½ teaspoon ancho chile powder
 ½ teaspoon dried oregano

 1 top sirloin steak, 1¾ to 2 pounds and about
   1¼ inches thick
   Extra-virgin olive oil
 1 lime, quartered

1. Prepare the grill for direct cooking over medium heat (350° to 450°F).

2. In a small bowl mix the rub ingredients.

3. Lightly coat the steak on both sides with oil and season evenly with the rub. Allow the steak to stand at room temperature for 15 to 30 minutes before grilling.

4. Brush the cooking grates clean. Grill the steak over ***direct medium heat***, with the lid closed as much as possible, until cooked to your desired doneness, 10 to 12 minutes for medium rare, turning once or twice (if flare-ups occur, move the steak temporarily over indirect heat). Remove from the grill and let rest for 3 to 5 minutes.

5. Cut the steak across the grain into thin slices. Serve warm with lime wedges. Serving suggestion: Corn and Tomato Summer Salad (for recipe, see page 121).

SERVES: 4 to 6

SIRLOIN STEAK
MARINATED IN CURRY AND COCONUT

PREP TIME: 10 minutes
MARINATING TIME: 3 to 4 hours
GRILLING TIME: 10 to 12 minutes

Marinade
- 1 cup unsweetened coconut milk, stirred
- ½ cup roughly chopped yellow onion
- 3 tablespoons fresh lime juice
- 1 tablespoon Madras-style curry powder
- 2 teaspoons soy sauce
- 2 garlic cloves

- 1 top sirloin steak, 1½ to 2 pounds and about 1¼ inches thick

1. In a blender combine the marinade ingredients and process until the onion is finely chopped. Using a sharp knife, lightly score the surface of the steak in a crosshatch pattern with shallow slashes no more than ⅛ inch deep. Place the steak in a 13x9-inch glass dish and pour in the marinade. Turn the steak to coat both sides, cover, and refrigerate for 3 to 4 hours, turning the steak once or twice.

2. Allow the steak to stand at room temperature for 15 to 30 minutes before grilling.

3. Prepare the grill for direct cooking over medium heat (350° to 450°F).

4. Remove the steak from the dish, allowing most of the marinade to drip back into the dish. Discard the marinade.

5. Brush the cooking grates clean. Grill the steak over ***direct medium heat***, with the lid closed as much as possible, until cooked to your desired doneness, 10 to 12 minutes for medium rare, turning once or twice (if flare-ups occur, move the steak temporarily over indirect heat). Remove from the grill and let rest for 3 to 5 minutes.

6. Cut the steak across the grain into thin slices. Serve warm.

SERVES: 4 to 6

TERIYAKI SIRLOIN KABOBS
WITH BELL PEPPERS AND PINEAPPLE

PREP TIME: 30 minutes
MARINATING TIME: 1 hour
GRILLING TIME: 6 to 8 minutes
SPECIAL EQUIPMENT: 8 metal or bamboo skewers (if using bamboo, soak in water for at least 30 minutes)

Marinade

- ¼ cup extra-virgin olive oil
- ¼ cup soy sauce
- ¼ cup packed brown sugar
- 2 tablespoons rice wine (mirin)
- 1 large whole shallot, grated
- 1 tablespoon sesame seeds
- 1 tablespoon grated fresh ginger
- 2 garlic cloves, grated or minced
- 1 teaspoon toasted sesame oil
- 1 teaspoon ground black pepper

- 1 top sirloin steak, about 1½ pounds and 1 to 1¼ inches thick, cut into 1½-inch cubes
- 1 teaspoon kosher salt
- ½ small red onion, cut in half and separated into leaves
- 1 red bell pepper, cut into 1½-inch squares
- ½ fresh pineapple, cut into 1½-inch cubes

1. In a medium bowl whisk the marinade ingredients. Add the meat to the bowl and turn to coat all sides. Cover and refrigerate for 1 hour.

2. Prepare the grill for direct cooking over high heat (450° to 550°F).

3. Remove the meat from the bowl, pat dry, and season with the salt. Put the onion leaves and pepper squares in the bowl of marinade and turn to coat evenly. Thread the meat onto skewers and the vegetables and pineapple alternately onto their own skewers.

4. Brush the cooking grates clean. Grill the meat kabobs over *direct high heat*, with the lid closed as much as possible, until the outside of the meat is dark and caramelized, 6 to 8 minutes for medium rare, turning once or twice (if flare-ups occur, move the meat temporarily over indirect heat). At the same time, grill the vegetable and pineapple kabobs over *direct high heat* until tender, 6 to 8 minutes, turning occasionally. Remove the kabobs from the grill and serve warm.

SERVES: 4

SIRLOIN AND CHERRY TOMATO KABOBS

WITH CREAMY POLENTA

PREP TIME: 20 minutes
MARINATING TIME: 1 to 4 hours
GRILLING TIME: 6 to 8 minutes
SPECIAL EQUIPMENT: 12 metal or bamboo skewers (if using bamboo, soak in water for at least 30 minutes)

Marinade
¼ cup extra-virgin olive oil
2 tablespoons chopped fresh rosemary leaves
1 teaspoon crushed red pepper flakes
1 teaspoon ground black pepper

1 top sirloin steak, about 1½ pounds and 1 to 1¼ inches thick, cut into 1½-inch cubes

Polenta
3–4 cups whole milk or water
2 teaspoons kosher salt
½ cup dry polenta
2 tablespoons unsalted butter

2½ teaspoons kosher salt
1½ pints large cherry tomatoes
Extra-virgin olive oil

1. In a medium bowl whisk the marinade ingredients. Add the meat and turn to coat evenly. Cover the bowl and refrigerate for 1 to 4 hours.

2. In a medium saucepan over high heat, bring 3 cups of the milk to a simmer (do not boil). Add the salt, reduce the heat to medium-low, and add the polenta in a thin stream, whisking constantly to prevent the polenta from clumping. Bring back to a simmer, reduce the heat to low and continue cooking, whisking frequently, until the polenta is cooked and has a loose, porridge-like consistency. Stir in the butter, turn off the heat, and set aside.

3. Prepare the grill for direct cooking over high heat (450° to 550°F).

4. Remove the meat from the bowl and discard the marinade. Season evenly with the salt. Thread the meat onto skewers and the tomatoes onto their own skewers. Lightly brush the tomatoes with oil.

5. Brush the cooking grates clean. Grill the meat kabobs over **_direct high heat_**, with the lid closed as much as possible, until cooked to your desired doneness, 6 to 8 minutes for medium rare, turning once or twice (if flare-ups occur, move the kabobs temporarily over indirect heat). At the same time, grill the tomato kabobs over **_direct high heat_** until lightly charred and heated through, 3 to 4 minutes, turning occasionally. Remove the kabobs from the grill as they are done.

6. If the polenta has cooled, place it over medium heat until it is warmed through, adding ½ to 1 cup of milk, if necessary, stirring frequently. Serve the kabobs warm with the polenta.

SERVES: 4

PERUVIAN SIRLOIN SKEWERS
WITH PEPPERS AND ONIONS

PREP TIME: 30 minutes
MARINATING TIME: 2 hours
GRILLING TIME: 8 to 12 minutes
SPECIAL EQUIPMENT: metal or bamboo skewers
(if using bamboo, soak in water for at least
30 minutes)

Marinade
- 2 medium jalapeño chile peppers
- 1 cup coarsely chopped red onion
- ½ cup extra-virgin olive oil
- ¼ cup red wine vinegar
- 1 tablespoon paprika
- 4 garlic cloves
- 2 teaspoons kosher salt
- 1½ teaspoons ground cumin

- 1 top sirloin steak, about 1½ pounds and 1 to 1¼ inches thick, cut into strips about ¾ inch wide
- 2 medium red bell peppers, cut into 1- to 1½-inch squares
- 1 large red onion, cut lengthwise in half through the core, each half cut into 6 wedges

1. Remove and discard the stems, whitish veins, and seeds of the jalapeños, and then put the jalapeños in the bowl of a food processor. Add the remaining marinade ingredients and process until smooth. Set aside ¼ cup of the marinade for the bell peppers and onion.

2. Place the steak in a large, resealable plastic bag and pour in the marinade. Press the air out of the bag and seal tightly. Turn the bag to distribute the marinade, and refrigerate for 2 hours, turning occasionally.

3. Prepare the grill for direct cooking over medium heat (350° to 450°F).

4. Thread the bell peppers and onions alternately onto skewers. Brush with some of the reserved marinade. Thread the steak onto skewers, leaving some of the marinade on the meat. Discard the remaining marinade.

5. Brush the cooking grates clean. Grill the vegetable skewers over ***direct medium heat***, with the lid closed as much as possible, until lightly charred in spots and tender, 8 to 12 minutes, turning occasionally. At the same time, grill the steak skewers over ***direct medium heat*** until charred in spots and cooked to your desired doneness, 4 to 6 minutes for medium rare, turning once or twice (if flare-ups occur, move the skewers temporarily over indirect heat). Arrange the meat and vegetable skewers on plates and serve warm.

SERVES: 4

SPANISH SIRLOIN STEAK
WITH HORSERADISH-TARRAGON SAUCE

PREP TIME: 20 minutes
MARINATING TIME: 2 to 4 hours
GRILLING TIME: 10 to 12 minutes

Marinade
½ cup dry red wine
¼ cup extra-virgin olive oil
2 tablespoons red wine vinegar
1 tablespoon minced garlic
1 teaspoon dried oregano
1 teaspoon paprika
1 teaspoon kosher salt
½ teaspoon ground black pepper

1 top sirloin steak, 1¾ to 2 pounds and about
  1¼ inches thick

Sauce
½ cup sour cream
2 tablespoons prepared horseradish
1 tablespoon finely chopped fresh tarragon leaves
¼ teaspoon kosher salt
⅛ teaspoon ground black pepper

1. In a medium bowl whisk the marinade ingredients.

2. Place the steak in a large, resealable plastic bag and pour in the marinade. Press the air out of the bag and seal tightly. Turn the bag to distribute the marinade, place in a bowl, and refrigerate for 2 to 4 hours, turning occasionally.

3. In a medium bowl mix the sour cream and horseradish. Stir in the tarragon, salt, and pepper. Cover and refrigerate until ready to use.

4. Prepare the grill for direct cooking over medium heat (350° to 450°F).

5. Lift the steak from the bag, letting the excess marinade drip back into the bag. Discard the marinade. Allow the steak to stand at room temperature for 15 to 30 minutes before grilling.

6. Brush the cooking grates clean. Grill the steak over **direct medium heat**, with the lid closed as much as possible, until cooked to your desired doneness, 10 to 12 minutes for medium rare, turning once or twice (if flare-ups occur, move the steak temporarily over indirect heat). Remove from the grill and let rest for 3 to 5 minutes.

7. Cut the steak across the grain into thin slices. Serve warm with the sauce. Serving suggestion: Couscous Salad (for recipe, see page 123).

SERVES: 4 to 6

SIRLOIN STEAKS
WITH WASABI-GARLIC SAUCE

PREP TIME: 15 minutes, plus about 10 minutes for the sauce
MARINATING TIME: 2 to 4 hours
GRILLING TIME: 6 to 8 minutes

Marinade
  1 cup low-sodium soy sauce
  ¼ cup honey
  2 tablespoons fresh orange juice
  2 tablespoons chopped fresh cilantro leaves
  1 tablespoon fresh lime juice
  1 tablespoon chopped fresh mint leaves
  3 garlic cloves, minced
  1 teaspoon grated fresh ginger

  4 top sirloin steaks, each about 8 ounces and 1 inch thick

Sauce
  1½ cups heavy cream
  3 garlic cloves, minced
  2 tablespoons low-sodium soy sauce
  1 teaspoon cornstarch
  1 tablespoon fresh lime juice
  2 tablespoons prepared wasabi
  1 teaspoon Dijon mustard
  ½ teaspoon kosher salt

  1½ tablespoons extra-virgin olive oil

1. In a medium bowl whisk the marinade ingredients. Place the steaks in a large, resealable plastic bag and pour in the marinade. Press the air out of the bag and seal tightly. Turn the bag to distribute the marinade, and refrigerate for 2 to 4 hours, turning occasionally.

2. In a medium saucepan over medium heat, bring the cream and garlic to a simmer. Lower the heat and simmer for 5 minutes to reduce the cream slightly, stirring often (watch carefully so the cream does not boil over). In a small bowl combine the soy sauce with the cornstarch; stir until the cornstarch dissolves. Add the soy sauce mixture to the cream and simmer until the sauce is thickened slightly, about 2 minutes. Whisk in the lime juice, wasabi, and mustard and cook for 1 minute. Remove from the heat; season with the salt.

3. Allow the steaks to stand at room temperature for 15 to 30 minutes before grilling. Prepare the grill for direct cooking over high heat (450° to 550°F).

4. Remove the steaks from the bag and discard the marinade. Pat the steaks dry with paper towels. Brush both sides with the oil. Grill over **direct high heat**, with the lid closed as much as possible, until cooked to your desired doneness, 6 to 8 minutes for medium rare, turning once or twice (if flare-ups occur, move the steaks temporarily over indirect heat). Remove from the grill and let rest for 3 to 5 minutes. Serve warm with the sauce.

SERVES: 4

TRI-TIP STEAK SANDWICHES
WITH WHOLE-GRAIN MUSTARD SAUCE

PREP TIME: 20 minutes
MARINATING TIME: 1 hour
GRILLING TIME: 24 to 31 minutes

Paste
2 tablespoons whole-grain mustard
1 tablespoon finely chopped fresh rosemary leaves
1 tablespoon kosher salt
2 garlic cloves, minced
1 teaspoon ground black pepper

1 tri-tip roast, about 1½ pounds and 1½ inches thick, fat and silver skin removed

Sauce
2 tablespoons whole-grain mustard
2 tablespoons mayonnaise
1 tablespoon extra-virgin olive oil
1 teaspoon red wine vinegar
1 teaspoon kosher salt
½ teaspoon ground black pepper

8 slices sourdough bread, each about ½ inch thick
2 tablespoons unsalted butter, softened
1 bunch watercress

1. In a small bowl combine the paste ingredients. Rub the paste all over the roast, cover with plastic wrap, and refrigerate for 1 hour.

2. In a small bowl combine the sauce ingredients. Refrigerate until ready to use.

3. Allow the roast to stand at room temperature for 15 to 30 minutes before grilling.

4. Prepare the grill for direct and indirect cooking over medium heat (350° to 450°F).

5. Brush the cooking grates clean. Grill the roast over *direct medium heat* until well marked on both sides, 8 to 10 minutes, turning once or twice. Then move the roast over *indirect medium heat* and cook until it reaches your desired doneness, 15 to 20 minutes for medium rare, turning every 5 minutes or so. Keep the lid closed as much as possible during grilling. Remove from the grill and let rest for 5 to 10 minutes. Cut the roast across the grain into ¼-inch-thick slices.

6. Brush the bread with the butter and grill over *direct medium heat* until lightly toasted, about 1 minute, turning once.

7. Spread about 1 teaspoon of the sauce on 4 slices of bread, place a layer of the meat on top, and then some watercress. Top with the remaining bread slices.

SERVES: 4

PEPPERED TRI-TIP
WITH ROASTED PEPERONATA

PREP TIME: 30 minutes
GRILLING TIME: 35 to 45 minutes

Rub

1½ teaspoons kosher salt
1 teaspoon ground black pepper
1 teaspoon prepared chili powder
1 teaspoon granulated garlic

1 tri-tip roast, 2 to 2½ pounds and about
  1½ inches thick, fat and silver skin removed
  Extra-virgin olive oil

Peperonata

4 large bell peppers (red, yellow, or orange,
  or a mix)
3 tablespoons extra-virgin olive oil
2 tablespoons finely chopped fresh Italian
  parsley leaves
1 tablespoon red wine vinegar
¼ teaspoon kosher salt
¼ teaspoon ground black pepper

1. In a small bowl mix the rub ingredients. Lightly coat the roast all over with oil and season evenly with the rub, pressing it in gently so the rub adheres to the meat. Allow the roast to stand at room temperature for 15 to 30 minutes before grilling.

2. Prepare the grill for direct and indirect cooking over medium heat (350° to 450°F).

3. Brush the cooking grates clean. Grill the bell peppers over *direct medium heat*, with the lid closed as much as possible, until the skins are blackened and blistered all over, 12 to 15 minutes, turning occasionally. Place the peppers in a large bowl and cover with plastic wrap to trap the steam. Set aside for at least 10 minutes, then remove the peppers from the bowl and peel away and discard the charred skins, tops, and seeds. Cut the peppers into ½-inch strips and set aside. In a medium glass or stainless steel bowl, whisk the remaining peperonata ingredients. Add the peppers and mix well.

4. Grill the roast over *direct medium heat* until well marked on both sides, 8 to 10 minutes, turning once or twice. Move the roast over *indirect medium heat* and cook to your desired doneness, 15 to 20 minutes for medium rare, turning every 5 minutes or so. Keep the lid closed as much as possible during grilling. Remove from the grill and let rest for 5 to 10 minutes.

5. Cut the roast across the grain into ½-inch-thick slices. Drizzle any juices remaining on the cutting board over the slices, and serve warm with the peperonata on the side.

SERVES: 4 to 6

HICKORY TRI-TIP STEAK
WITH CHIVE CREAM SAUCE

PREP TIME: 20 minutes
GRILLING TIME: 23 to 30 minutes

1 tri-tip roast, 2 to 2½ pounds and about 1½ inches thick, fat and silver skin removed
Extra-virgin olive oil
1½ teaspoons kosher salt
¾ teaspoon ground black pepper

2 handfuls hickory wood chips, soaked in water for at least 30 minutes

Sauce

1 tablespoon unsalted butter
2 tablespoons minced shallot
2 teaspoons minced garlic
1½ cups heavy cream
2 tablespoons whole-grain mustard
½ teaspoon kosher salt
¼ teaspoon ground black pepper
2 tablespoons finely chopped fresh chives

1. Lightly coat the roast all over with oil and season with the salt and pepper. Allow to stand at room temperature for 15 to 30 minutes before grilling.

2. Prepare the grill for direct and indirect cooking over medium heat (350° to 450°F).

3. Brush the cooking grates clean. Drain and add the hickory wood chips directly onto burning coals or to the smoker box of a gas grill, following manufacturer's instructions.

4. Grill the roast over **direct medium heat** until well marked on both sides, 8 to 10 minutes, turning once or twice. Then move the roast over **indirect medium heat** and continue cooking until it reaches your desired doneness, 15 to 20 minutes for medium rare, turning every 5 minutes or so. Keep the lid closed as much as possible during grilling. Remove from the grill and let rest for 5 to 10 minutes while you make the sauce.

5. In a small saucepan over medium heat, melt the butter. Add the shallot and cook until soft but not browned, 1 to 2 minutes, stirring frequently. Add the garlic and cook just until fragrant, about 30 seconds, stirring frequently. Add the cream, mustard, salt, and pepper. Mix well and bring to a simmer (do not let the sauce boil). Simmer until the sauce is reduced to a consistency that is thick and coats the back of a spoon, about 5 minutes. Add the chives.

6. Cut the roast across the grain into thin slices. Serve warm with the sauce on the side.

SERVES: 4 to 6

TRI-TIP AND ZUCCHINI SKEWERS
WITH SMOKED PAPRIKA AIOLI

PREP TIME: 20 minutes
GRILLING TIME: 4 to 6 minutes
SPECIAL EQUIPMENT: 10 metal or bamboo skewers (if using bamboo, soak in water for at least 30 minutes)

Aioli
- 1 cup mayonnaise
- 3 tablespoons fresh lemon juice
- 1½ tablespoons finely chopped fresh Italian parsley leaves
- 5 large garlic cloves, minced
- 2 teaspoons smoked paprika
- ¼ teaspoon ground black pepper

Skewers
- 1 pound beef tips (also called tri-tip), cut into 1-inch chunks
- 3 medium zucchini, cut crosswise into ½-inch-thick slices
- 2 tablespoons extra-virgin olive oil
- 1½ teaspoons kosher salt
- 1 teaspoon smoked paprika
- ¼ teaspoon ground black pepper

1. In a medium glass or stainless steel bowl, whisk the aioli ingredients. Keep chilled until ready to use. (The aioli may be prepared one day in advance.)

2. Prepare the grill for direct cooking over medium heat (350° to 450°F).

3. In a large bowl combine the skewer ingredients and toss gently. Thread the steak and zucchini pieces on their own skewers, making sure to skewer the zucchini through the peel so that as much surface area as possible will be touching the grill. Do not crowd the ingredients.

4. Brush the cooking grates clean. Grill the steak kabobs over ***direct medium heat***, with the lid closed as much as possible, until nicely charred, 4 to 6 minutes, turning once or twice (if flare-ups occur, move the kabobs temporarily over indirect heat). Grill the zucchini kabobs at the same time over ***direct medium heat*** until nicely charred and crisp-tender, 4 to 6 minutes, turning once or twice. Remove from the grill and let rest for 3 to 5 minutes. Serve warm with the aioli.

SERVES: 4

FLATIRON STEAKS
WITH HERB BUTTER AND GRILLED BROCCOLINI

PREP TIME: 15 minutes
CHILLING TIME: about 1 hour
GRILLING TIME: 11 to 15 minutes

Butter

- ½ cup (1 stick) unsalted butter, softened
- 1 tablespoon finely chopped fresh tarragon leaves
- 1 tablespoon finely chopped fresh chives
- 1 garlic clove, grated or minced
- ½ teaspoon finely grated lemon zest
- ½ teaspoon kosher salt

- 4 flatiron steaks, each 6 to 8 ounces and about 1 inch thick, excess fat and any gristle removed
  Extra-virgin olive oil
  Kosher salt
  Ground black pepper

- 1 pound broccolini, with stalks no wider than ½ inch
- 1 teaspoon crushed red pepper flakes

1. In a small bowl combine the butter ingredients. Scoop the mixture out of the bowl onto a sheet of parchment or waxed paper. Loosely shape the mixture into a log about 1 inch in diameter. Roll the log in the paper and twist the ends in opposite directions to form an even cylinder. Refrigerate for at least 1 hour, or until the butter is chilled.

2. Lightly brush the steaks on both sides with oil and season evenly with salt and pepper. Allow the steaks to stand at room temperature for 15 to 30 minutes before grilling. In a large bowl of water, submerge the broccolini for 20 to 30 minutes so that they absorb water. This will help them steam a little on the grill.

3. Prepare the grill for direct and indirect cooking over high heat (450° to 550°F).

4. Pour off the water from the bowl of broccolini. Lightly drizzle some oil over the broccolini and season with salt and the red pepper flakes. Toss to coat evenly.

5. Brush the cooking grates clean. Grill the steaks over **direct high heat**, with the lid closed as much as possible, until cooked to your desired doneness, 6 to 8 minutes for medium rare, turning once or twice (if flare-ups occur, move the steaks temporarily over indirect heat). Remove from the grill and let rest while you grill the broccolini.

6. Using tongs, lift the broccolini and allow any excess oil to drip back into the bowl. Grill the broccolini over ***direct high heat***, with the lid closed as much as possible, until lightly charred, 3 to 4 minutes, turning occasionally. Finish cooking over ***indirect high heat*** for 2 to 3 minutes.

7. Cut four ½-inch-thick pieces of butter and place one in the center of each steak. Serve warm with the broccolini.

SERVES: 4

CITRUS-MARINATED FLATIRON KABOBS
WITH SCALLIONS

PREP TIME: 15 minutes
GRILLING TIME: 6 to 8 minutes
SPECIAL EQUIPMENT: metal or bamboo skewers
(if using bamboo, soak in water for at least
30 minutes)

Paste

- ½ cup loosely packed fresh mint leaves
- ½ cup loosely packed fresh Italian parsley leaves
  and tender stems
- ½ cup fresh orange juice
- 2 tablespoons fresh lime juice
- 2 tablespoons extra-virgin olive oil
- 3 garlic cloves
- ½ jalapeño chile pepper, with seeds
- 1½ teaspoons kosher salt
- ½ teaspoon ground cumin
- ½ teaspoon prepared chili powder
- ¼ teaspoon ground black pepper

- 4 flatiron steaks, each 6 to 8 ounces and about
  1 inch thick, excess fat and any gristle removed,
  cut into 1½-inch pieces
- 12 scallions (white and light green parts only),
  cut into 1½-inch pieces
  Extra-virgin olive oil

1. In a food processor combine the paste ingredients and process until smooth.

2. Put the steak pieces in a large glass or stainless steel bowl. Add the paste and mix well to coat the pieces evenly. Allow to stand at room temperature for 15 to 30 minutes before grilling.

3. Prepare the grill for direct cooking over high heat (450° to 550°F).

4. Skewer the steak and scallion pieces, alternating the ingredients. Lightly brush with oil.

5. Brush the cooking grates clean. Grill the kabobs over **_direct high heat_**, with the lid closed as much as possible, until the meat is cooked to your desired doneness, 6 to 8 minutes for medium rare, turning once or twice (if flare-ups occur, move the kabobs temporarily over indirect heat). Remove from the grill and let rest for 3 to 5 minutes. Serve warm.

SERVES: 4

FLATIRON STEAK BURRITOS
WITH BLACK BEAN SALSA

PREP TIME: 30 minutes
GRILLING TIME: 10 to 13 minutes

Rub

½ teaspoon chipotle chile powder
½ teaspoon ground cumin
½ teaspoon kosher salt
¼ teaspoon ground black pepper

1 flatiron steak, about 1 pound and 1 inch thick, excess fat and any gristle removed
Extra-virgin olive oil

Salsa

2 cups diced ripe tomatoes
1 can (15 ounces) black beans, rinsed
¼ cup roughly chopped fresh cilantro leaves
2 tablespoons extra-virgin olive oil
1 scallion (white and light green parts only), thinly sliced
1 serrano chile pepper or small jalapeño chile pepper, seeds and stems removed, minced
1 teaspoon fresh lime juice
¼ teaspoon ground cumin
¼ teaspoon chipotle chile powder
Kosher salt
Ground black pepper

6 flour tortillas (10 inches)
1½ cups shredded romaine lettuce
1 cup grated Monterey Jack or cheddar cheese
1 cup sour cream (optional)

1. In a small bowl mix the rub ingredients. Lightly brush the steak on both sides with oil and season evenly with the rub. Allow the steak to stand at room temperature for 15 to 30 minutes before grilling.

2. Prepare the grill for direct cooking over medium heat (350° to 450°F).

3. In a large skillet over medium heat, combine the salsa ingredients and cook until the beans are warm and the liquid just begins to simmer, 2 to 4 minutes, stirring occasionally. Season with salt and pepper.

4. Brush the cooking grates clean. Grill the steak over *direct medium heat*, with the lid closed as much as possible, until cooked to your desired doneness, 8 to 10 minutes for medium rare, turning once or twice (if flare-ups occur, move the steak temporarily over indirect heat). Transfer the steak to a cutting board and let rest for 3 to 5 minutes.

5. Roll up the tortillas into a cylinder, and then wrap the tortillas in foil. Warm over *direct medium heat* for 2 to 3 minutes, rolling occasionally. Reheat the salsa in the skillet over medium heat.

6. Cut the steak in half lengthwise and then cut the steak across the grain into very thin slices. Lay out the warm tortillas on a work surface. Divide the salsa evenly over the bottom half of each tortilla. Top with steak slices, lettuce, and cheese. If desired, top with sour cream. Fold the bottom edge up and over the filling, tucking it in as tight as possible. Fold in the edges and roll up each burrito. Serve warm.

SERVES: 4 to 6

MISO-MARINATED FLATIRON STEAKS
WITH SHIITAKE MUSHROOMS

PREP TIME: 10 minutes
MARINATING TIME: 1 to 2 hours
GRILLING TIME: 6 to 8 minutes
SPECIAL EQUIPMENT: 12-inch skillet

Marinade
- ¼ cup miso
- ¼ cup sake or light beer
- 2 tablespoons hot water
- 1 tablespoon brown sugar
- 4 garlic cloves, minced

- 4 flatiron steaks, each 6 to 8 ounces and about 1 inch thick, excess fat and any gristle removed

Mushrooms
- 2 tablespoons unsalted butter
- 2 tablespoons extra-virgin olive oil
- ½ pound shiitake mushrooms, cleaned, stems removed
- 4 large garlic cloves, thinly sliced
- ¼ teaspoon kosher salt
- ⅛ teaspoon ground black pepper
- 1 teaspoon rice vinegar

1. In a small bowl whisk the marinade ingredients. Place the steaks in a glass or stainless steel dish and pour in the marinade, turning the steaks to coat both sides. Cover and refrigerate for 1 to 2 hours, turning the steaks once or twice.

2. Remove the steaks from the dish and discard the marinade. Allow the steaks to stand at room temperature for 15 to 30 minutes before grilling.

3. Prepare the grill for direct cooking over medium heat (350° to 450°F).

4. Brush the cooking grates clean. Grill the steaks over **_direct medium heat_**, with the lid closed as much as possible, until cooked to your desired doneness, 6 to 8 minutes for medium rare, turning once or twice (if flare-ups occur, move the steaks temporarily over indirect heat). Remove from the grill and let rest while you cook the mushrooms.

5. In a 12-inch skillet over high heat, melt the butter with the oil. Add the mushrooms and spread them out in a single layer so that most of them are touching the bottom of the skillet. Cook without moving them for 2 minutes. Stir the mushrooms, and then add the garlic, salt, and pepper. Cook until the mushrooms are barely tender, 2 to 3 minutes, stirring two or three times. Add the vinegar. Mix well.

6. Serve the steaks warm with the hot mushrooms. Serving suggestion: Pickled Cucumbers (for recipe, see page 123).

SERVES: 4

104

EASY CHUCK STEAK SANDWICHES

WITH SWEET CHILI SAUCE

PREP TIME: 10 minutes
GRILLING TIME: 1¼ to 1½ hours
SPECIAL EQUIPMENT: large disposable foil pan

Rub

- 1 tablespoon prepared chili powder
- 1 teaspoon kosher salt
- ½ teaspoon granulated garlic
- ½ teaspoon granulated onion

2–3 chuck steaks, about 1 inch thick, 2 to 2½ pounds total
Extra-virgin olive oil

Sauce

- 1 bottle (12 ounces) ketchup-style chili sauce
- 2 tablespoons molasses
- 2 tablespoons Worcestershire sauce

- 6 hamburger buns

1. In a small bowl mix the rub ingredients. Lightly brush the steaks on both sides with oil and season evenly with the rub. Allow the steaks to stand at room temperature for 15 to 30 minutes before grilling.

2. Prepare the grill for direct cooking over high heat (450° to 550°F).

3. In a medium bowl mix the sauce ingredients.

4. Brush the cooking grates clean. Sear the steaks over *direct high heat*, with the lid closed as much as possible, for 6 to 7 minutes, turning once or twice. Transfer the steaks to the foil pan, overlapping them if needed. Pour the sauce over the steaks.

5. Adjust the grill for direct and indirect cooking over medium heat (350° to 450°F).

6. Place the pan over *direct medium heat* and let the sauce come to a simmer. Then slide the pan over *indirect medium heat*, tightly cover with foil, and cook until the steaks are fork tender, 1 to 1½ hours. Check the sauce every 30 minutes and, if it becomes too thick, add a little water. Keep the lid closed as much as possible during grilling. Remove the pan from the grill. Let the steaks rest in the sauce for about 5 minutes. Transfer the steaks to a cutting board and coarsely chop them. Return the chopped meat to the sauce and stir to combine.

7. Toast the buns, cut sides down, over *direct medium heat*, until warmed and grill marks appear, about 1 minute. Heap the meat on the buns and serve warm.

SERVES: 4 to 6

HANGER STEAKS
WITH BUTCHER'S BIG RED SAUCE

PREP TIME: 10 minutes, plus 10 to 20 minutes for the sauce
GRILLING TIME: 10 to 14 minutes

Sauce
½ cup finely chopped red onion
2 tablespoons finely chopped shallot
2 tablespoons extra-virgin olive oil
1 cup low-sodium beef broth
¼ cup steak sauce, preferably A.1.®
¼ cup ketchup
¼ teaspoon ground black pepper

Rub
1 teaspoon kosher salt
½ teaspoon ground black pepper
½ teaspoon granulated garlic
½ teaspoon prepared chili powder

4 hanger steaks, each 6 to 8 ounces and 1½ to 2 inches thick
Extra-virgin olive oil

NOTE!
Whole hanger steaks typically weigh 1½ to 2 pounds and are 1½ to 2 inches thick. Running down the middle of each steak is a tendon that holds the two sides of the steak together. Some butchers cut along both sides of the tendon and remove most of it for you, creating two strips of meat from one whole steak. If you happen to find a whole steak (only one per animal), remove the tendon yourself before grilling.

1. In a medium saucepan over medium heat, combine the onion, shallot, and oil. Cook until the onion is golden brown, 5 to 8 minutes, stirring occasionally to prevent burning. Add the remaining sauce ingredients, mix well, and simmer until you have about 1 cup of sauce remaining, 5 to 10 minutes. Remove the saucepan from the heat and let the sauce cool for about 5 minutes. Then puree the sauce in a food processor or blender.

2. In a small bowl mix the rub ingredients. Lightly brush the steaks on both sides with oil and season evenly with the rub. Allow the steaks to stand at room temperature for 15 to 30 minutes before grilling.

3. Prepare the grill for direct cooking over medium heat (350° to 450°F).

4. Brush the cooking grates clean. Grill the steaks over ***direct medium heat***, with the lid closed as much as possible, until cooked to your desired doneness, 10 to 14 minutes for medium rare, turning once or twice (if flare-ups occur, move the steaks temporarily over indirect heat). Remove from the grill and let rest for 3 to 5 minutes.

5. Serve the steaks whole or cut them into thin slices. Serve warm with the sauce. Serving suggestion: Twice-Grilled Potatoes (for recipe, see page 119).

SERVES: 4

HANGER STEAKS
WITH GRUYÈRE-SHALLOT FONDUE

PREP TIME: 30 minutes
GRILLING TIME: 10 to 14 minutes

Steaks

- 4 hanger steaks, each 6 to 8 ounces and 1½ to 2 inches thick
- 2 teaspoons extra-virgin olive oil
- 2 teaspoons kosher salt
- ¾ teaspoon ground black pepper

Fondue

- 1 tablespoon unsalted butter
- 2 tablespoons minced shallot
- ¼ cup dry white wine
- ¼ cup low-sodium beef broth
- 1 teaspoon white wine vinegar
- 2 cups grated Gruyère cheese (about 8 ounces)
- 1 tablespoon cornstarch
- 1 tablespoon cognac or brandy
- ¾ teaspoon chopped fresh thyme leaves
- ⅛ teaspoon ground black pepper

- 4 fresh thyme sprigs for garnish (optional)

1. Prepare the grill for direct cooking over medium heat (350° to 450°F).

2. Lightly brush the steaks on both sides with the oil and season evenly with the salt and pepper. Allow the steaks to stand at room temperature for 15 to 30 minutes before grilling.

3. In a medium saucepan over medium heat, melt the butter. Add the shallot and cook until tender, about 2 minutes, stirring occasionally. Add the wine, broth, and vinegar, and bring to a boil over high heat. Remove from the heat and set aside.

4. Brush the cooking grates clean. Grill the steaks over **_direct medium heat_**, with the lid closed as much as possible, until cooked to your desired doneness, 10 to 14 minutes for medium rare, turning once or twice (if flare-ups occur, move the steaks temporarily over indirect heat). Remove from the grill and let rest while finishing the fondue.

You will have the smoothest fondue if you melt the cheese one handful at a time and stir, stir, stir.

5. In a medium bowl toss the cheese and cornstarch together. Return the wine mixture to a boil over high heat. Reduce the heat to low. Stirring constantly, add the cheese to the wine mixture a handful at a time. Let each addition melt completely before adding the next. Cook just until the fondue comes to a boil. Stir in the cognac, thyme, and pepper. Remove from the heat.

6. Transfer each steak to an individual plate. Top each with equal amounts of the fondue and a thyme sprig, if using. Serve warm. Serving suggestion: Basic Grilled Asparagus (for recipe, see page 112).

SERVES: 4

Sides

110

112 Basic Grilled Asparagus

113 Asparagus with Sherry-Bacon Vinaigrette

114 Eggplant with Spicy Asian Dressing

114 Acorn Squash with Brown Butter and Garlic

115 Artichokes with Oregano and Salt

116 Melted Onions

117 Grilled Carrots

118 Glazed Sweet Potatoes

118 Mashed Sweet Potatoes with Grilled Onions

119 Twice-Grilled Potatoes

120 Corn on the Cob with Basil-Parmesan Butter

120 Cajun Corn with Louisiana Butter

121 Corn and Tomato Summer Salad

121 Roasted Corn and Black Bean Salad

122 Grilled Vegetable and Orzo Salad

123 Couscous Salad

123 Pickled Cucumbers

124 Skillet Corn Bread with Bacon and Chives

125 Grilled Garlic Bread

125 Smoky Sweet Baked Beans

Sides

BASIC GRILLED ASPARAGUS

PREP TIME: 5 minutes
GRILLING TIME: 6 to 8 minutes

 1 pound asparagus
 2 tablespoons extra-virgin olive oil
 ½ teaspoon kosher salt

1. Prepare the grill for direct cooking over medium heat (350º to 450ºF).

2. Remove and discard the tough bottom of each asparagus spear by grasping each end and bending it gently until it snaps at its natural point of tenderness, usually two-thirds of the way down the spear. Using a vegetable peeler, peel off the outer skin from the bottom half of each remaining spear.

3. Spread the asparagus on a large plate. Drizzle the oil and salt over the top. Turn the spears until they are evenly coated.

4. Brush the cooking grates clean. Grill the asparagus (perpendicular to the grate) over ***direct medium heat***, with the lid closed as much as possible, until browned in spots but not charred, 6 to 8 minutes, turning occasionally. Serve warm or at room temperature.

SERVES: 4

ASPARAGUS WITH SHERRY-BACON VINAIGRETTE

PREP TIME: 15 minutes
GRILLING TIME: 6 to 8 minutes

4–6 slices bacon
1 teaspoon finely chopped fresh thyme leaves
½ teaspoon minced garlic
1 tablespoon sherry vinegar
¼ teaspoon kosher salt
¼ teaspoon ground black pepper
1 pound asparagus
½ small red onion, thinly sliced crosswise

NOTE!

Look for firm asparagus stalks with deep green or purplish tips. Also check the bottom of the spears. If they are dried up, chances are they have been sitting around for too long. Thicker spears fare better on the grill.

1. Prepare the grill for direct cooking over medium heat (350° to 450°F).

2. In a medium skillet over medium heat, lay the bacon in a single layer and cook until crispy, 8 to 10 minutes, turning occasionally. Drain the bacon on paper towels, reserving the bacon fat in the skillet.

3. Pour off all but 3 tablespoons of the bacon fat and return the skillet over medium heat. Add the thyme and garlic to the skillet and let them sizzle for about 10 seconds. Add the vinegar, salt, and pepper, and then remove the skillet from the heat.

4. Remove and discard the tough bottom of each asparagus spear by grasping each end and bending it gently until it snaps at its natural point of tenderness, usually two-thirds of the way down the spear. Using a vegetable peeler, peel off the outer skin from the bottom half of each remaining spear. Put the asparagus on a plate or platter. Pour the vinaigrette over the asparagus. Turn the asparagus to coat evenly. Finely chop the drained bacon.

5. Brush the cooking grates clean. Grill the asparagus over *direct medium heat*, with the lid closed as much as possible, until browned in spots but not charred, 6 to 8 minutes, turning occasionally. Arrange the asparagus on a serving platter. Sprinkle the bacon over the asparagus. Arrange the onion slices on top. Serve warm or at room temperature.

SERVES: 4

Sides

EGGPLANT WITH SPICY ASIAN DRESSING

PREP TIME: 10 minutes
GRILLING TIME: 8 to 10 minutes

Dressing
1–2 serrano chile peppers, stems and seeds removed, minced
3 tablespoons soy sauce
2 tablespoons fresh lemon juice
2 tablespoons minced yellow onion
1 tablespoon water

2 globe eggplants, each about 12 ounces
Vegetable oil
1 teaspoon granulated garlic

1. Prepare the grill for direct cooking over medium heat (350° to 450°F).

2. In a small glass or stainless steel bowl, combine the dressing ingredients.

3. Cut the eggplants crosswise into ½-inch slices. Generously brush both sides of the slices with oil and season evenly with the granulated garlic.

4. Brush the cooking grates clean. Grill the eggplant slices over **direct medium heat**, with the lid closed as much as possible, until well marked and tender, 8 to 10 minutes, turning once. Place the slices on a platter and spoon the dressing over the top. Serve warm.

SERVES: 4

ACORN SQUASH WITH BROWN BUTTER AND GARLIC

PREP TIME: 10 minutes
GRILLING TIME: 40 minutes to 1 hour

Glaze
3 tablespoons unsalted butter, cut into 3 pieces
2 tablespoons dark brown sugar
2 teaspoons minced garlic
1 teaspoon kosher salt
¼ teaspoon ground black pepper
¼ teaspoon grated nutmeg
1 tablespoon cider vinegar

2 small acorn squashes, each about 1½ pounds

1. In a small saucepan or skillet, combine the glaze ingredients except the vinegar. Cook over medium-high heat for 2 to 3 minutes, stirring occasionally. Remove from the heat; cool to room temperature.

2. Prepare the grill for indirect cooking over high heat (450° to 550°F).

3. Using a large knife, carefully cut the squashes in half lengthwise. Scoop out and discard the seeds and strings. Add the vinegar to the cooled glaze. Brush the glaze over the exposed flesh of the squashes.

4. Brush the cooking grates clean. Grill the squashes, with the exposed flesh facing up, over **indirect high heat**, with the lid closed as much as possible, until a sharp knife inserted all the way into the flesh slides out easily, 40 minutes to 1 hour, basting occasionally with the glaze that pools in the bowl of the squashes. Remove from the grill and serve warm.

SERVES: 4

ARTICHOKES WITH OREGANO AND SALT

PREP TIME: 30 minutes
GRILLING TIME: 4 to 6 minutes

    4 large artichokes, 10 to 12 ounces each
       Juice of 1 lemon
    1 tablespoon extra-virgin olive oil
    ½ teaspoon dried oregano
    ¼ teaspoon granulated garlic
    ¼ teaspoon kosher salt
    ½ cup (1 stick) unsalted butter, melted

1. Bring a large pot of salted water to a boil.

2. Cut the stem off of each artichoke, leaving about ½ inch attached. Peel off the dark outer leaves until you expose the light green, yellowish leaves underneath. Lay each artichoke on its side and cut off the top half so you have just the firm base to work with. Cut each base in half lengthwise through the stem and drop each half into a large glass or stainless steel bowl of water mixed with the lemon juice (to prevent discoloration).

3. One at a time, lift the artichokes from the water and use a teaspoon to scoop out all of the fuzzy choke and purplish leaves. Cook the artichokes in the boiling, salted water until you can pierce them easily with a knife, 10 to 12 minutes, but don't overcook them or they will fall apart on the grill. Drain the artichokes in a colander and place in a large bowl. While still warm, add the oil, oregano, granulated garlic, and salt. Toss gently to coat the artichokes. (The artichokes may be made up to this point and refrigerated for up to 4 hours. Bring to room temperature before grilling.)

4. Prepare the grill for direct cooking over medium heat (350° to 450°F).

5. Brush the cooking grates clean. Grill the artichokes over *direct medium heat*, with the lid closed as much as possible, until well browned and warm, 4 to 6 minutes, turning once. Serve warm with the melted butter.

SERVES: 4

MELTED ONIONS

PREP TIME: 25 minutes
GRILLING TIME: 1¼ to 1¾ hours, for charcoal grills only
SPECIAL EQUIPMENT: large disposable foil pan

- 6 medium yellow onions (skin on), 8 to 10 ounces each, about the size of a tennis ball
- ¼ cup (½ stick) unsalted butter
- ½ teaspoon kosher salt
- ¼ teaspoon ground black pepper
- 1 teaspoon sherry vinegar
- 1 tablespoon minced fresh Italian parsley leaves

1. Fill a chimney starter to the rim with charcoal and burn the charcoal until it is lightly covered with ash. Spread the charcoal in a tightly packed, single layer across one-half of the charcoal grate. Let the coals burn down to medium heat (350° to 450°F). Leave all the vents open.

2. With the onions still in their skins, place them on the charcoal grate against the charcoal. Close the lid and cook the onions until very tender, 1 to 1½ hours. Occasionally swap the positions of the onions for even cooking and turn the blackened skins away from the charcoal. When very tender, the onions will be blackened in spots all over and a knife blade will slide in and out of each onion like it is a ripe peach. Some onions may take longer than others.

3. At this point, to finish cooking the onions, you will need to add more charcoal to the fire for medium heat.

4. Remove the onions from the grill and let cool completely. Carefully remove the skin from each onion, being careful to leave the root ends intact so they hold the layers of the onions together. Cut each onion lengthwise through the stem and root end.

5. When the fire is ready, put the cooking grate in place. In a large disposable foil pan over **direct medium heat**, melt the butter. Carefully add the onions in a single layer and season with the salt and pepper. Using tongs, turn the onions in the butter to coat them.

6. Slide the pan over **indirect medium heat** and cook, with the lid closed as much as possible, until the onions are very tender and just beginning to brown, 10 to 15 minutes, carefully turning the onions once or twice. If desired, to keep the onions warm, cover the pan with foil and let the onions continue to cook over indirect heat for as long as 30 minutes. Wearing barbecue mitts, remove the pan from the grill. Splash the vinegar and sprinkle the parsley over the onions. Serve warm.

SERVES: 4 to 6

GRILLED CARROTS

PREP TIME: 10 minutes
GRILLING TIME: 3 to 5 minutes

- 8 medium carrots, each 6 to 8 inches long and about 1 inch wide at the thick end
- ¼ cup (½ stick) unsalted butter
- ½ teaspoon red wine vinegar
- ¼ teaspoon ground nutmeg
- ½ teaspoon kosher salt, divided
- ¼ teaspoon ground black pepper, divided
- 1 teaspoon minced fresh Italian parsley leaves (optional)

1. Peel the carrots and cook them in boiling water until they are partially cooked but still crisp, 4 to 6 minutes. Drain the carrots and rinse them under cold water for at least 10 seconds to stop the cooking.

2. Prepare the grill for direct cooking over high heat (450° to 550°F).

3. Lay the carrots flat on a work surface. In a small saucepan over medium heat, melt the butter with the vinegar and nutmeg. Brush the carrots with about half the butter mixture and season them with about half the salt and pepper.

4. Brush the cooking grates clean. Grill the carrots over *direct high heat*, with the lid open, until lightly charred with spots and stripes, 3 to 5 minutes, turning occasionally. Move the carrots to a platter, brush them with the remaining butter mixture, and season them with the remaining salt and pepper. Sprinkle the parsley over the top, if using. Serve warm.

SERVES: 4

Sides

GLAZED SWEET POTATOES

PREP TIME: 10 minutes
GRILLING TIME: 15 to 20 minutes

Glaze

Grated zest of 2 limes
¼ cup fresh lime juice
¼ cup canola oil
2 tablespoons honey
½ teaspoon kosher salt
¼ teaspoon ground black pepper

2 sweet potatoes, about 2 pounds total

1. Prepare the grill for direct cooking over medium heat (350° to 450°F).

2. In a small glass or stainless steel bowl, whisk the glaze ingredients. Peel the sweet potatoes, trim the ends, and cut each potato into ½-inch slices. Brush the potatoes on both sides with the glaze.

3. Brush the cooking grates clean. Grill the potatoes over *direct medium heat*, with the lid closed as much as possible, until they are easily pierced with a knife, 15 to 20 minutes, turning and brushing them with the glaze about every 5 minutes. Remove from the grill and serve warm.

SERVES: 4 to 6

MASHED SWEET POTATOES WITH GRILLED ONIONS

PREP TIME: 10 minutes
GRILLING TIME: about 1¼ hours

4 sweet potatoes, about 4 pounds total, scrubbed
1 large yellow onion, cut crosswise into ½-inch slices
Extra-virgin olive oil
Kosher salt
Ground black pepper
¼ cup (½ stick) unsalted butter, softened

1. Prepare the grill for direct and indirect cooking over medium heat (350° to 450°F).

2. Brush the cooking grates clean. Grill the sweet potatoes over *indirect medium heat*, with the lid closed as much as possible, until tender when pierced with a fork, about 1 hour, turning three or four times. Remove from the grill and allow to cool. When cool enough to handle, cut the potatoes in half lengthwise. Remove and discard the skins. Place the potatoes in a medium bowl and cover with aluminum foil.

3. Brush the onion slices with oil and season evenly with salt and pepper. Grill over *direct medium heat*, with the lid closed as much as possible, for 10 to 12 minutes, turning once. Remove from the grill and allow to cool, and then cut into ¼-inch dice.

4. Using a heavy-duty mixer or potato masher, mash the potatoes with the butter until smooth. Add the diced onion and mix well. Serve warm.

SERVES: 8 to 10

TWICE-GRILLED POTATOES

PREP TIME: 15 minutes
GRILLING TIME: 40 to 45 minutes

  4 russet potatoes, about 10 ounces each,
     scrubbed and halved lengthwise
     Vegetable oil

Stuffing

  ¾ cup sour cream
  ½ cup minced cooked ham
1½ cups grated Gruyère cheese, divided
  2 teaspoons Dijon mustard
     Kosher salt
     Ground black pepper

1. Prepare the grill for direct cooking over medium heat (350° to 450°F).

2. Lightly coat the potato halves with oil. Brush the cooking grates clean. Grill the potatoes over *direct medium heat*, with the lid closed as much as possible, until tender when pierced with a fork, 30 to 35 minutes, turning three or four times. Allow to cool slightly.

3. When cool enough to handle, use a small sharp knife to cut around the cut side of the potato to within ¼ inch of the skin. Using a teaspoon or melon baller, scoop out the interior of the potato leaving a shell about ¼ inch thick. Place the potato pulp in a large bowl. Set the potato shells aside while preparing the stuffing.

4. Using a potato masher or pastry blender, mash the potato pulp in the bowl. Add the sour cream and mix well. Stir in the ham and half of the cheese. Add the mustard, and season with salt and pepper. Taste and adjust the seasoning, adding more mustard, if desired. Divide the stuffing evenly among the skins, so that the stuffing mounds slightly. Sprinkle the remaining cheese over the stuffing.

5. Grill the stuffed potatoes over *direct medium heat*, with the lid closed, until the cheese is melted and the potatoes are heated through, about 10 minutes. Serve immediately.

SERVES: 8

Sides

CORN ON THE COB WITH BASIL-PARMESAN BUTTER

PREP TIME: 10 minutes
GRILLING TIME: 10 to 15 minutes

Butter
- ¼ cup (½ stick) unsalted butter, softened
- ¼ cup freshly grated Parmigiano-Reggiano® cheese
- 2 tablespoons finely chopped fresh basil leaves
- ½ teaspoon kosher salt
- ¼ teaspoon ground black pepper
- ¼ teaspoon granulated garlic

- 4 ears fresh corn, husked

1. Prepare the grill for direct cooking over medium heat (350° to 450°F).

2. In a small bowl mash the butter ingredients with the back of a fork, and then stir to distribute the seasonings throughout the butter.

3. Brush about 1 tablespoon of the seasoned butter all over each ear of corn. Brush the cooking grates clean. Grill the corn over **_direct medium heat_**, with the lid closed as much as possible, until browned in spots and tender, 10 to 15 minutes, turning occasionally. Serve warm with the remaining butter spread on the corn.

SERVES: 4

CAJUN CORN WITH LOUISIANA BUTTER

PREP TIME: 15 minutes
GRILLING TIME: 25 to 30 minutes

Butter
- 1 teaspoon paprika
- ½ teaspoon onion powder
- ½ teaspoon kosher salt
- ½ teaspoon dried thyme
- ¼ teaspoon dried oregano
- ⅛ teaspoon ground cayenne pepper
- ¼ cup (½ stick) unsalted butter, softened

- 4 ears fresh corn, in their husks

1. Prepare the grill for direct cooking over medium heat (350° to 450°F).

2. In a small bowl combine the butter ingredients, stirring to distribute the seasonings evenly.

3. Pull back the husks on each ear of corn, leaving the husks attached at the stem. Remove and discard the corn silk. Evenly spread about 1 tablespoon of the seasoned butter over the kernels of each ear. Fold the husks back around the kernels. Using string or a thin strip of corn husk, tie the husks at the top.

4. Brush the cooking grates clean. Grill the corn over **_direct medium heat_**, with the lid closed as much as possible, until the kernels are tender, 25 to 30 minutes, turning three or four times. Don't worry if the husks brown or burn. Carefully pull the husks back. Remove the husks with a knife. Serve warm.

SERVES: 4

CORN AND TOMATO SUMMER SALAD

PREP TIME: 10 minutes

- 1 tablespoon minced shallot
- 2 teaspoons sherry vinegar
- ½ teaspoon Dijon mustard
- ½ teaspoon kosher salt
- ¼ teaspoon ground black pepper
- 2 tablespoons extra-virgin olive oil
- 2 ears fresh corn, husked
- ½ cup cherry tomatoes, cut into quarters
- ¼ cup finely chopped fresh basil leaves

1. In a medium glass or stainless steel bowl, whisk the shallot, vinegar, mustard, salt, and pepper. Slowly whisk in the oil to create a smooth vinaigrette.

2. Place the corn in a large pot of boiling salted water. Turn off the heat, cover the pot, and allow to cook until barely tender, 4 to 5 minutes. Remove from the water and allow to cool. Cut the kernels off the cobs and add to the vinaigrette. Add the tomatoes and basil. Stir to combine. Serve at room temperature.

SERVES: 4

ROASTED CORN AND BLACK BEAN SALAD

PREP TIME: 15 minutes
GRILLING TIME: 10 to 15 minutes

- 3 ears fresh corn, husked
  Extra-virgin olive oil
  Kosher salt
- 2 cans (15 ounces each) black beans, rinsed
- 1½ cups roughly chopped ripe tomatoes
- ½ cup finely chopped celery
- 2 tablespoons finely chopped fresh cilantro leaves

Dressing

- 3 tablespoons extra-virgin olive oil
  Finely grated zest and juice of 1 lime
- 1 teaspoon minced garlic
- ½ teaspoon ground cumin
- ½ teaspoon kosher salt
- ¼ teaspoon ground black pepper

1. Prepare the grill for direct cooking over medium heat (350° to 450°F).

2. Lightly brush the corn all over with oil and season with salt. Brush the cooking grates clean. Grill the corn over ***direct medium heat***, with the lid closed as much as possible, until browned in spots and tender, 10 to 15 minutes, turning occasionally.

3. In a large glass bowl cut the kernels off the cobs. Add the beans, tomatoes, celery, and cilantro.

4. In a small bowl whisk the dressing ingredients. Pour the dressing over the salad and mix to coat evenly. Serve at room temperature.

SERVES: 6 to 8

Sides

GRILLED VEGETABLE AND ORZO SALAD

PREP TIME: 20 minutes, plus about 10 minutes for the orzo
GRILLING TIME: 12 to 15 minutes

- 8 ounces orzo pasta
- 6 tablespoons extra-virgin olive oil
- 2 tablespoons balsamic vinegar
- 2 teaspoons minced garlic
- 2 teaspoons Dijon mustard
  Kosher salt
  Ground black pepper
- 2 ears fresh corn, husked
- 2 medium zucchini, halved lengthwise
- 1 medium red bell pepper, quartered and seeded
- 1 cup grape tomatoes or small cherry tomatoes
- 4 ounces feta cheese, crumbled
- ¼ cup roughly chopped fresh Italian parsley or basil leaves

1. Prepare the grill for direct cooking over medium heat (350° to 450°F).

2. Cook the orzo according to package directions. Drain and set aside in a large glass or stainless steel bowl.

3. In a small glass or stainless steel bowl, whisk the oil, vinegar, garlic, mustard, 1 teaspoon salt, and 1 teaspoon pepper until smooth. Lightly coat the corn, zucchini, and bell pepper with about half of the olive oil mixture. Reserve the remaining half for dressing the salad.

4. Brush the cooking grates clean. Grill the vegetables over **_direct medium heat_**, with the lid closed as much as possible, until lightly charred and crisp-tender, turning as needed. The corn will take 12 to 15 minutes and the zucchini and pepper will take 4 to 6 minutes. Remove the vegetables from the grill as they are done. Set aside to cool.

5. Cut the kernels off the cobs into the bowl of orzo. Use the back of a knife to scrape the juice from the cobs. Scrape off and discard any burned pieces from the pepper quarters, and then cut the pepper and zucchini crosswise into ½-inch pieces. Add them to the bowl. Cut each tomato in half or into quarters, and add to the bowl along with the cheese and fresh herbs. Add as much of the remaining dressing as you like (you may not need all of it) and toss to coat. Season with salt and pepper. Serve at room temperature.

SERVES: 8

COUSCOUS SALAD

PREP TIME: 30 minutes

1½ cups quick-cooking couscous
⅓ cup raisins
2 cups chicken broth
¼ cup thinly sliced scallions (white part only)
3 tablespoons finely chopped fresh Italian parsley leaves
2 tablespoons finely chopped fresh mint leaves
2 tablespoons extra-virgin olive oil
2 tablespoons fresh lemon juice
½ teaspoon kosher salt
¼ teaspoon ground black pepper

1. In a large saucepan combine the couscous and raisins. Heat the broth to boiling and pour it over the couscous. Toss lightly to mix, cover, and allow to stand for 20 minutes.

2. In a small bowl mix the rest of the ingredients together. Add the mixture to the couscous. Fluff and toss gently with a fork to combine. Serve warm.

SERVES: 4

PICKLED CUCUMBERS

PREP TIME: 10 minutes
PICKLING TIME: about 2 hours

¼ cup rice vinegar
1 tablespoon fresh lemon juice
1 tablespoon granulated sugar
1 teaspoon kosher salt
¼ cup water
2 thin Japanese cucumbers, 4 to 6 ounces each

1. In a medium glass or stainless steel bowl, mix the vinegar, lemon juice, sugar, and salt until the sugar and salt are dissolved. Add the water.

2. Cut the cucumbers into thin strips, each about ¼ inch wide and 3 inches long (could be any shape, really). Add the cucumbers to the pickling liquid and set aside at room temperature for 2 hours, stirring the cucumbers a few times. Drain the pickles before serving and arrange them in a medium serving bowl.

SERVES: 4 to 6

Sides

SKILLET CORN BREAD WITH BACON AND CHIVES

PREP TIME: 20 minutes
GRILLING TIME: 20 to 30 minutes
SPECIAL EQUIPMENT: 10-inch nonstick, ovenproof skillet

4 slices bacon
2 cups yellow cornmeal
1½ cups all-purpose flour
½ cup granulated sugar
1 teaspoon baking powder
1 teaspoon baking soda
1 teaspoon kosher salt
¼ teaspoon ground black pepper
¼ teaspoon ground cayenne pepper
2 tablespoons finely chopped fresh chives
3 large eggs
1 cup milk
¼ cup sour cream

1. In a 10-inch nonstick, ovenproof skillet over medium heat, lay the bacon flat and cook until crispy, 10 to 12 minutes, turning occasionally. Drain the bacon on paper towels. Pour off and discard all but 2 tablespoons of bacon fat in the skillet.

2. Prepare the grill for indirect cooking over medium heat (350° to 450°F).

3. In a large bowl combine the cornmeal, flour, sugar, baking powder, baking soda, salt, black pepper, and cayenne pepper. Finely chop the drained bacon and add it to the bowl along with the chives. Mix well. In another large bowl combine the eggs, milk, and sour cream. Whisk to break up the eggs. Pour the milk mixture into the cornmeal mixture. Mix with a wooden spoon until well combined.

4. Pour the corn bread batter into the skillet with the bacon fat and spread it out evenly. Brush the cooking grates clean. Grill over *indirect medium heat*, with the lid closed as much as possible, until it is golden brown around the edges and a toothpick inserted in the center comes out clean, 20 to 30 minutes, rotating the pan occasionally for even cooking. Allow to cool completely in the skillet. Invert the corn bread onto a cutting board. Cut into wedges. Serve at room temperature.

SERVES: 8

GRILLED GARLIC BREAD

PREP TIME: 10 minutes
GRILLING TIME: about 10 minutes

Butter
- ½ cup (1 stick) unsalted butter, softened
- 1 tablespoon minced garlic
- ½ teaspoon kosher salt
- ½ teaspoon paprika

- 1 loaf Italian or French bread, cut in half lengthwise

- 1 tablespoon finely chopped fresh Italian parsley leaves

1. Prepare the grill for direct cooking over medium heat (350° to 450°F).

2. In a medium bowl mix the butter ingredients until evenly incorporated.

3. Spread the butter evenly over the cut sides of the bread. Grill the bread, cut sides down, over **direct medium heat**, with the lid open, until toasted, 1 to 2 minutes. Remove from the grill and cut the bread into pieces, each about 2 inches thick. Sprinkle parsley over the bread just before serving.

SERVES: 6 to 8

SMOKY SWEET BAKED BEANS

PREP TIME: 15 minutes
GRILLING TIME: 25 to 28 minutes
SPECIAL EQUIPMENT: large ovenproof saucepan

- 4 ounces bacon, cut into ½-inch pieces
- ½ cup finely chopped yellow onion
- 2 teaspoons minced garlic
- ¼ teaspoon crushed red pepper flakes
- 1 can (28 ounces) baked beans
- ¼ cup ketchup
- 2 teaspoons Worcestershire sauce
- ½ teaspoon prepared chili powder
  Kosher salt
  Ground black pepper

1. Prepare the grill for direct cooking over medium heat (350° to 450°F).

2. In a large ovenproof saucepan cook the bacon over **direct medium heat**, with the lid closed as much as possible, until crispy, 8 to 10 minutes, stirring occasionally. Add the onion and cook until tender, 2 to 3 minutes, stirring occasionally. Add the garlic and red pepper flakes, and cook for about 30 seconds, stirring occasionally. Add the baked beans (with their liquid), ketchup, Worcestershire sauce, and chili powder. Bring the mixture to a simmer, stirring occasionally.

3. Lower the temperature of the grill to low heat (250° to 350°F), and continue to cook the beans over **direct low heat**, with the lid closed as much as possible, for 15 minutes, stirring all the way to the bottom of the pot occasionally. Taste and adjust the seasoning with salt and pepper, if necessary. Serve warm.

SERVES: 4 to 6

Rubs

A rub is a mixture of spices, herbs, and other seasonings (often including sugar) that can quickly give a boost of flavors to foods before grilling. The next couple of pages provide some mighty good examples of rubs that work particularly well with steak. Try one when time is tight.

HOW LONG SHOULD I LEAVE A RUB ON MY STEAKS?

If you leave a rub on for a long time, the seasonings intermix with the juices in the meat and produce more pronounced flavors, as well as a crust. This is good to a point, but a rub with a lot of salt and sugar will draw moisture out of the meat over time, making the meat tastier, yes, but also drier. So how long should you use a rub? Here are some guidelines.

UP TO 15 MINUTES:	cubed steak for kabobs
15 TO 30 MINUTES:	steaks
30 MINUTES TO 1½ HOURS:	roasts
2 TO 8 HOURS:	big or tough cuts of meat

A WORD ABOUT FRESHNESS

Ground spices lose their aromas in a matter of months (eight to ten months maximum). If you have been holding onto a little jar of coriander for years, waiting to blend the world's finest version of curry powder, forget about it. Dump the old, tired coriander and buy some freshly ground. Better yet, buy whole coriander and grind the seeds yourself. Some people who are far more exacting than I am actually date each jar when they buy it. Whatever you do, store your spices in airtight containers away from light and heat, to give them a long, aromatic life.

RUB RECIPES FOR STEAK

Beef Rub
MAKES: about ¼ cup

- 4 teaspoons kosher salt
- 1 tablespoon pure chile powder
- 1 tablespoon granulated onion
- 1½ teaspoons granulated garlic
- 1 teaspoon paprika
- 1 teaspoon dried marjoram
- ½ teaspoon ground cumin
- ½ teaspoon ground black pepper
- ¼ teaspoon ground cinnamon

Classic Barbecue Spice Rub

MAKES: about ¼ cup

- 4 teaspoons kosher salt
- 2 teaspoons pure chile powder
- 2 teaspoons light brown sugar
- 2 teaspoons granulated garlic
- 2 teaspoons paprika
- 1 teaspoon celery seed
- 1 teaspoon ground cumin
- ½ teaspoon ground black pepper

Mexican Rub

MAKES: about ¼ cup

- 1 tablespoon ground cumin
- 1 tablespoon brown sugar
- 2 teaspoons kosher salt
- 1 teaspoon pasilla or pure chile powder
- 1 teaspoon ground coriander
- 1 teaspoon dried oregano

Asian Rub

MAKES: about ¼ cup

- 2 tablespoons paprika
- 2 teaspoons kosher salt
- 2 teaspoons ground coriander
- 2 teaspoons Chinese five-spice powder
- 1 teaspoon ground ginger
- ½ teaspoon ground allspice
- ½ teaspoon ground cayenne pepper

Pick-Me-Up Pepper Rub

SPECIAL EQUIPMENT: spice mill
MAKES: 1½ tablespoons

- 1 teaspoon whole black peppercorns
- 1 teaspoon mustard seed
- 1 teaspoon paprika
- ½ teaspoon granulated garlic
- ½ teaspoon kosher salt
- ½ teaspoon light brown sugar
- ½ teaspoon ground cayenne pepper

1. Crush the peppercorns and mustard seed in a spice mill. Transfer to a small bowl and combine with the remaining ingredients.

Type-A Rub

MAKES: 2 tablespoons

- 1 teaspoon dry mustard
- 1 teaspoon granulated onion
- 1 teaspoon paprika
- 1 teaspoon kosher salt
- ½ teaspoon granulated garlic
- ½ teaspoon ground coriander
- ½ teaspoon ground cumin
- ½ teaspoon ground black pepper

Rubs

Southwest Rub
MAKES: about ¼ cup

- 2 teaspoons pure chile powder
- 2 teaspoons granulated garlic
- 2 teaspoons paprika
- 2 teaspoons kosher salt
- 1 teaspoon ground coriander
- 1 teaspoon ground cumin
- 1 teaspoon ground black pepper

Espresso-Chile Rub
SPECIAL EQUIPMENT: spice mill
MAKES: about ¼ cup

- 2 tablespoons dark-roast coffee or espresso beans
- 2 teaspoons cumin seed, toasted
- 1 tablespoon ancho chile powder
- 1 teaspoon paprika
- 1 teaspoon kosher salt
- 1 teaspoon ground black pepper

1. In a spice mill pulse the coffee beans and cumin seed until finely ground. Transfer to a small bowl, add the remaining ingredients, and stir to combine.

Caribbean Rub
MAKES: about ¼ cup

- 1 tablespoon light brown sugar
- 1 tablespoon granulated garlic
- 1 tablespoon dried thyme
- 2¼ teaspoons kosher salt
- ¾ teaspoon ground black pepper
- ¾ teaspoon ground allspice

Cajun Rub
MAKES: about 3 tablespoons

- 2 teaspoons finely chopped fresh thyme leaves
- 1½ teaspoons kosher salt
- 1 teaspoon granulated garlic
- 1 teaspoon granulated onion
- 1 teaspoon paprika
- 1 teaspoon light brown sugar
- ¾ teaspoon ground black pepper
- ¼ teaspoon ground cayenne pepper

Tarragon Rub
MAKES: about ¼ cup

- 1½ tablespoons dried tarragon
- 2½ teaspoons kosher salt
- 2 teaspoons ground black pepper
- 1½ teaspoons dried thyme
- 1 teaspoon rubbed sage, packed

Marinades

Marinades work more slowly than rubs, but they can seep in a little deeper. Typically a marinade is made with some acidic liquid, some oil, and some combination of herbs and spices. These ingredients can fill in the gaps when a particular cut of meat lacks enough taste or richness. They can also give food characteristics that reflect regional and ethnic cooking styles.

HOW LONG SHOULD I MARINATE?

The right times vary depending on the strength of the marinade and the food you are marinating. If your marinade includes intense ingredients, such as soy sauce, liquor, or hot chiles and spices, don't overdo it. If an acidic marinade is left too long on meat, it can make the surface mushy or dry. Here are some general guidelines to get you going.

15 TO 30 MINUTES:	cubed steak for kabobs
1 TO 3 HOURS:	steaks
2 TO 6 HOURS:	roasts
6 TO 12 HOURS:	big or tough cuts of meat

NOTE

Marinades work faster at room temperature, but if the food requires more than 30 minutes of marinating time, put it in the refrigerator.

TIPS

When the marinade includes an acid, be sure to use non-reactive containers. These are dishes made of glass, plastic, stainless steel, or ceramic. Containers made of aluminum or metals other than stainless steel react with acids and add a metallic flavor to food. My favorite container is a resealable plastic bag. I set the bag in a bowl so the liquid comes up the sides of the food and covers it evenly. If there is not enough liquid, I turn the bag over every so often.

After a marinade has been in contact with raw meat, either discard it or boil it for at least 1 minute. The boiling will destroy any harmful bacteria that might have been left by the meat. A boiled marinade often works well as a basting sauce, too.

Lots of people do it but never admit to it…. Go ahead. Use that bottled Italian dressing as a marinade. It is actually pretty good, and when you are pressed for time and need to make dinner fast after a busy day, it will work just fine. I won't tell.

Marinades

MARINADE RECIPES FOR STEAK

Teriyaki Marinade
MAKES: about 2 cups

- 1 cup pineapple juice
- ½ cup low-sodium soy sauce
- ½ cup finely chopped yellow onion
- 1 tablespoon toasted sesame oil
- 1 tablespoon grated fresh ginger
- 1 tablespoon minced garlic
- 1 tablespoon dark brown sugar
- 1 tablespoon fresh lemon juice

Spicy Cayenne Marinade
MAKES: about ½ cup

- ¼ cup extra-virgin olive oil
- 2 tablespoons fresh lemon juice
- 1 tablespoon minced garlic
- 2 teaspoons dried oregano
- 2 teaspoons paprika
- 1½ teaspoons kosher salt
- 1 teaspoon celery seed
- 1 teaspoon ground cayenne pepper

Bourbon Marinade
MAKES: about 1 cup

- ½ cup bourbon
- ¼ cup ketchup
- 2 tablespoons extra-virgin olive oil
- 2 tablespoons soy sauce
- 1 tablespoon white wine vinegar
- 2 teaspoons minced garlic
- ½ teaspoon Tabasco® sauce
- ½ teaspoon ground black pepper

North Indian Marinade
MAKES: about 1½ cups

- 1 cup plain yogurt
- 3 tablespoons fresh lemon juice
- 1 tablespoon paprika
- 2 teaspoons minced garlic
- 2 teaspoons minced jalapeño chile pepper, with seeds
- 1 teaspoon ground cumin
- 1 teaspoon curry powder
- 1 teaspoon kosher salt
- ½ teaspoon ground ginger
- ½ teaspoon ground coriander

Tequila-Orange Marinade

MAKES: about 1 cup

½ cup loosely packed fresh mint leaves
½ cup loosely packed fresh Italian parsley leaves
  and tender stems
½ cup fresh orange juice
2 tablespoons tequila
2 tablespoons extra-virgin olive oil
2 medium garlic cloves, crushed
2 teaspoons minced jalapeño chile peppers,
  without seeds
1½ teaspoons kosher salt
½ teaspoon ground cumin
½ teaspoon pure chile powder
¼ teaspoon ground black pepper

1. In a food processor combine the ingredients and process until smooth.

Magical Mediterranean Marinade

MAKES: about ½ cup

2 tablespoons extra-virgin olive oil
2 tablespoons chopped fresh rosemary leaves
1 tablespoon chopped fresh thyme leaves
1 tablespoon minced shallot
1 tablespoon balsamic vinegar
1 tablespoon whole-grain mustard
1 teaspoon minced garlic
1 teaspoon kosher salt
1 teaspoon ground black pepper

Cuban Marinade

MAKES: about 2 cups

½ cup fresh orange juice
½ cup fresh lemonade
½ cup finely chopped yellow onion
¼ cup extra-virgin olive oil
2 tablespoons minced garlic
2 tablespoons dried oregano
2 tablespoons fresh lime juice

Greek Marinade

MAKES: about ½ cup

6 tablespoons extra-virgin olive oil
3 tablespoons red wine vinegar
½ teaspoon minced garlic
½ teaspoon kosher salt
½ teaspoon dried oregano
¼ teaspoon crushed red pepper flakes

Sweet Soy Marinade

MAKES: about 1½ cups

¾ cup soy sauce
½ cup rice wine (mirin)
¼ cup ketchup
2 tablespoons rice vinegar
2 teaspoons minced garlic
1 teaspoon toasted sesame oil

Sauces

Sauces open up a world of flavors for grillers. They offer us almost limitless ways for distinguishing our food and making it more interesting. Once you have learned some of the fundamentals about balancing flavors and some of the techniques for holding sauces together, you are ready to develop your own. The next couple of pages provide some tasty examples of sauces that work particularly well with steak.

SAUCE RECIPES FOR STEAK

Siren Steak Sauce
MAKES: about ⅔ cup

½ cup water
½ cup dry red wine
½ cup ketchup
¼ cup dark molasses
2 tablespoons red wine vinegar
1 tablespoon Dijon mustard
1 tablespoon Worcestershire sauce
½ teaspoon pure chile powder
½ teaspoon celery seed
½ teaspoon kosher salt
¼ teaspoon curry powder
¼ teaspoon ground cumin

1. In a medium saucepan combine the ingredients. Mix well. Bring to a simmer over medium heat and cook, uncovered, stirring occasionally, until about ⅔ cup remains, about 30 minutes. Allow to cool to room temperature.

Classic Red Barbecue Sauce
MAKES: about 1¼ cups

¾ cup apple juice
½ cup ketchup
3 tablespoons cider vinegar
2 teaspoons soy sauce
1 teaspoon Worcestershire sauce
1 teaspoon molasses
½ teaspoon pure chile powder
½ teaspoon granulated garlic
¼ teaspoon ground black pepper

1. In a small saucepan mix the ingredients. Simmer for a few minutes over medium heat, and then remove the saucepan from the heat.

Weber's Tangy Barbecue Sauce
MAKES: about 1⅓ cups

½ cup chopped celery
3 tablespoons chopped onion
2 tablespoons unsalted butter
1 cup ketchup
¼ cup fresh lemon juice
2 tablespoons granulated sugar
2 tablespoons cider vinegar
1 tablespoon Worcestershire sauce
1 teaspoon dry mustard
⅛ teaspoon ground black pepper

1. In a medium saucepan over medium heat, cook the celery and onion in butter until tender. Add the remaining ingredients and bring to a boil. Reduce the heat, cover, and simmer for 15 minutes. Serve warm.

Tomato Salsa
MAKES: about 2 cups

- 1½ cups finely diced ripe tomatoes
- ½ cup finely diced white onion, rinsed in a sieve under cold water
- 2 tablespoons finely chopped fresh cilantro leaves
- 1 tablespoon extra-virgin olive oil
- 2 teaspoons fresh lime juice
- 1 teaspoon minced jalapeño chile pepper, with seeds
- ¼ teaspoon dried oregano
- ¼ teaspoon kosher salt
- ¼ teaspoon ground black pepper

1. In a medium glass or stainless steel bowl, mix the ingredients. If desired, to fully incorporate the flavors, let the salsa sit at room temperature for about 1 hour. Drain in a sieve just before serving.

Creamy Horseradish Sauce
MAKES: about 1 cup

- ¾ cup sour cream
- 2 tablespoons prepared horseradish
- 2 tablespoons finely chopped fresh Italian parsley leaves
- 2 teaspoons Dijon mustard
- 2 teaspoons Worcestershire sauce
- ½ teaspoon kosher salt
- ¼ teaspoon ground black pepper

1. In a medium bowl thoroughly mix the ingredients. Cover and refrigerate until about 30 minutes before serving.

Lemon-Parsley Butter
MAKES: about ¼ cup

- ¼ cup (½ stick) unsalted butter, softened
- 1 tablespoon finely chopped fresh Italian parsley leaves
- ¼ teaspoon finely grated lemon zest
- 1 teaspoon fresh lemon juice
- ¼ teaspoon kosher salt
- ¼ teaspoon ground black pepper

1. In a small glass or stainless steel bowl, combine the ingredients. Using the back of a fork, mash and stir until the ingredients are evenly distributed. Cover and refrigerate until ready to serve.

Tapenade
MAKES: about ½ cup

- ¾ cup black olives, such as kalamata or other imported olives, pitted
- 2 anchovy fillets (oil-packed), drained
- 2 tablespoons coarsely chopped shallot
- 2 tablespoons extra-virgin olive oil
- 1 tablespoon fresh lemon juice
- 1 tablespoon capers, drained
- 1 teaspoon minced garlic
- ¼ teaspoon ground black pepper

1. In a food processor combine the ingredients and process to make a spreadable paste. Cover and refrigerate in a glass or stainless steel bowl for up to 1 week.

Grilling Guide for Steaks

The following cuts, weights, and grilling times are meant to be guidelines rather than hard and fast rules. Cooking times are affected by such factors as altitude, wind, and outside temperature. Two rules of thumb: Grill steaks and kabobs using the direct method for the time given on the chart or to your desired doneness, turning once or twice. Grill thicker steaks using both the direct and indirect methods for the time given on the chart or until an instant-read thermometer reaches the desired internal temperature. Let steaks rest for 3 to 5 minutes before carving. The internal temperature of the meat will rise by 5 to 10 degrees during this time. All cooking times are for medium-rare doneness.

BEEF	THICKNESS/WEIGHT	APPROXIMATE GRILLING TIME
Steak: New York strip, porterhouse, rib-eye, T-bone, and filet mignon (tenderloin)	¾ inch thick	**4 to 6 minutes** direct high heat
	1 inch thick	**6 to 8 minutes** direct high heat
	1¼ inches thick	**8 to 10 minutes** direct high heat
	1½ inches thick	**10 to 14 minutes**: sear 6 to 8 minutes direct high heat, grill 4 to 6 minutes indirect high heat
Flank	1½ to 2 pounds, ¾ inch thick	**8 to 10 minutes** direct medium heat
Flatiron	1 inch thick	**8 to 10 minutes** direct medium heat
Hanger	1 inch thick	**8 to 10 minutes** direct medium heat
Kabob	1- to 1½-inch cubes	**4 to 6 minutes** direct high heat
Skirt	¼ to ½ inch thick	**4 to 6 minutes** direct high heat
Tri-tip	2 to 2½ pounds	**30 to 40 minutes**: sear 10 minutes direct medium heat, grill 20 to 30 minutes indirect medium heat

WHEN IS IT DONE?

For optimal safety, the USDA recommends cooking red meat to 145°F (final temperature) and ground red meat to 160°F. The USDA believes that 145°F is medium rare, but virtually all chefs today believe medium rare is closer to 130°F. The chart to the right compares chef standards with USDA recommendations. Ultimately, it is up to you what doneness you choose.

DONENESS	CHEF STANDARDS	USDA
Rare	120° to 125°F	n/a
Medium rare	125° to 135°F	145°F
Medium	135° to 145°F	160°F
Medium well	145° to 155°F	n/a
Well done	155°F +	170°F

Checking for the doneness of steaks is a little difficult with an instant-read thermometer because you need to position the sensing "dimple" of the probe right in the center of the meat. It's easy to miss the center and get an inaccurate reading, so learn to use the "touch test." Most raw steaks are as soft as the fleshiest part of your thumb when your hand is relaxed. As they cook, the steaks get firmer and firmer. (1) If you press your middle finger and thumb together and press the fleshiest part of your thumb, the firmness is very close to that of a medium-rare steak. (2) If you are still not sure of the doneness, take the steak off the grill and put the best-looking side (presentation side) facing down on a cutting board. With the tip of a sharp knife, make a little cut in the middle so you can see the color of the meat inside. If the color is still too red, put it back on the grill. Otherwise, get the rest of the steaks off the grill and pat yourself on the back. (3) Before you serve the steaks, feel their firmness and remember that for the next time you use the touch test.

Grilling Guide for Veggies

GRILL WHAT'S GROWING AT THE TIME

Vegetables in season locally have big advantages over whatever has been shipped from across the world. They are riper, so they taste better. That means you can grill them simply with great results.

EXPOSE AS MUCH SURFACE AREA AS POSSIBLE

Cut each vegetable to give you the biggest area to put in direct contact with the cooking grates. The more direct contact, the better the flavors will be. For example, choose peppers with flat sides that you can easily slice off the core. The flatter the sides, the more surface area will caramelize on the hot cooking grates.

USE THE GOOD OIL

Vegetables need oil to prevent sticking and burning. Neutral oils like canola oil will do the job fine, but an extra-virgin olive oil provides the added benefit of improving the flavor of virtually every vegetable. Brush on just enough to coat each side thoroughly but not so much that the vegetables would drip oil and cause flare-ups. Season the vegetables generously with salt and pepper (some of it will fall off). For more flavors, marinate the vegetables at room temperature for 20 minutes to an hour in olive oil, vinegar, garlic, herbs, and spices.

WHEN IS IT DONE?

I like firm vegetables such as onions and fennel to be somewhere between crisp and tender. If you want them softer, grill them a few minutes longer, although watch them carefully for burning. The grill intensifies the sweetness of vegetables quickly and that can lead to burning. Cut the vegetables as evenly as you can. A ½-inch thickness is right for most of them.

Just about everything from artichokes to zucchini tends to cook best over direct medium heat. The temperature on the grill's thermometer should be somewhere between 350° and 450°F. If any parts get a little too dark, turn the vegetables over. Otherwise turn them as few times as possible.

VEGETABLES	THICKNESS/SIZE	APPROXIMATE GRILLING TIME
Artichoke (10 to 12 ounces)	whole	**14 to 18 minutes:** boil 10 to 12 minutes; cut in half and grill 4 to 6 minutes direct medium heat
Asparagus	½-inch diameter	**6 to 8 minutes** direct medium heat
Bell pepper	whole	**10 to 15 minutes** direct medium heat
Bell/Chile pepper	¼-inch slices	**6 to 8 minutes** direct medium heat
Carrot	1-inch diameter	**7 to 11 minutes:** boil 4 to 6 minutes, grill 3 to 5 minutes direct high heat
Corn, husked		**10 to 15 minutes** direct medium heat
Corn, in husk		**25 to 30 minutes** direct medium heat
Eggplant	½-inch slices	**8 to 10 minutes** direct medium heat
Fennel	¼-inch slices	**10 to 12 minutes** direct medium heat
Garlic	whole	**45 minutes to 1 hour** indirect medium heat
Mushroom, shiitake or button		**8 to 10 minutes** direct medium heat
Mushroom, portabello		**10 to 15 minutes** direct medium heat
Onion	halved	**35 to 40 minutes** indirect medium heat
	½-inch slices	**8 to 12 minutes** direct medium heat
Potato	whole	**45 minutes to 1 hour** indirect medium heat
	½-inch slices	**14 to 16 minutes** direct medium heat
Potato, new	halved	**15 to 20 minutes** direct medium heat
Scallion	whole	**3 to 4 minutes** direct medium heat
Squash, acorn	1½ pounds, halved	**40 minutes to 1 hour** indirect medium heat
Sweet potato	whole	**50 minutes to 1 hour** indirect medium heat
	¼-inch slices	**8 to 10 minutes** direct medium heat
Tomato, garden or plum	halved	**6 to 8 minutes** direct medium heat
	whole	**8 to 10 minutes** direct medium heat
Zucchini	½-inch slices	**3 to 5 minutes** direct medium heat
	halved	**4 to 6 minutes** direct medium heat

Safety

Please read your owner's guide and familiarize yourself with and follow all "dangers," "warnings," and "cautions." Also follow the grilling procedures and maintenance requirements contained in your owner's guide. If you cannot locate the owner's guide for your grill model, please contact the manufacturer prior to use.

If you have any questions concerning the "dangers," "warnings," and "cautions" contained in your Weber® gas or charcoal owner's guide, or if you do not have an owner's guide for your specific grill model, please contact Weber-Stephen Products Co. Customer Service at 1.800.446.1071 before using your grill. You can also access your owner's guide online at www.weber.com.

GENERAL NOTES

1. Grills radiate a lot of heat, so always keep the grill at least five feet away from any combustible materials, including the house, garage, deck rails, etc. Combustible materials include, but are not limited to, wood or treated wood decks, wood patios, or wood porches. Never use a grill indoors or under a covered patio.

2. Keep the grill in a level position at all times.

3. Use proper barbecuing tools with long, heat-resistant handles.

4. Don't wear loose or highly flammable clothing when grilling.

5. Do not leave infants, children, or pets unattended near a hot grill.

6. Use barbecue mitts to protect hands while cooking or adjusting the vents.

GAS GRILL SAFETY

1. Always keep the bottom tray and grease catch pan of your gas grill clean and free of debris. This not only prevents dangerous grease fires, it deters visits from unwanted critters.

2. If a flare-up should occur, make sure the lid is closed. Then, if necessary, move the food over indirect heat until the flare-up subsides. Never use water to extinguish flames on a gas grill.

3. Do not line the funnel-shaped bottom tray with foil. This could prevent grease from flowing into the grease catch pan. Grease is also likely to catch in the tiny creases of the foil and start a fire.

4. Never store propane tanks or spares indoors (that means the garage, too).

5. For the first few uses, the temperature of a new gas grill may run hotter than normal. Once your grill is seasoned and the inside of the cooking box is less reflective, the temperature will return to normal.

CHARCOAL GRILL SAFETY

1. Charcoal grills are designed for outdoor use only. If used indoors, toxic fumes will accumulate and cause serious bodily injury or death.

2. Do not add charcoal starter fluid or charcoal impregnated with charcoal starter fluid to hot or warm charcoal.

3. Do not use gasoline, alcohol, or other highly volatile fluids to ignite charcoal. If using charcoal starter fluid, remove any fluid that may have drained through the bottom vents before lighting the charcoal.

4. Do not use a grill unless all parts are in place. Make sure the ash catcher is properly attached to the legs underneath the bowl of the grill.

5. Remove the lid from the grill while lighting and getting the charcoal started.

6. Always put charcoal on top of the charcoal grate, not into the bottom of the bowl.

7. Do not place a chimney starter on or near any combustible surface.

8. Never touch the cooking or charcoal grate or the grill to see if it is hot.

9. Use the hook on the inside of the lid to hang the lid on the side of the bowl of the grill. Avoid placing a hot lid on carpet or grass. Do not hang the lid on the bowl handle.

10. To extinguish the coals, place the lid on the bowl and close all of the vents (dampers). Make sure that the vents on the lid and the bowl are completely closed. Do not use water, as it will damage the porcelain finish.

11. If a flare-up should occur, place the lid on the grill and close the top vent about halfway. If the flames are still threatening, open the lid and move the food over indirect heat. Do not use water to extinguish the flames.

12. Handle and store hot electric starters carefully. Do not place starters on or near any combustible surfaces.

13. Keep electrical cords away from the hot surfaces of the grill.

Index

A

Acorn Squash with Brown Butter and Garlic, 114
Aioli
    Olive, 78
    Smoked Paprika, 98
Ambassador Steaks with French Roast Spice Rub, 37
Argentinean-Style T-Bone Steaks with Salsa Criolla, 58
Artichokes with Oregano and Salt, 115
Arugula
    Basil-Arugula Pesto, 38
    Tagliata of Flank Steak with Arugula and Shaved Parmesan, 68
Asparagus
    Asparagus with Sherry-Bacon Vinaigrette, 113
    Basic Grilled Asparagus, 112
Avocados
    Avocado Sauce, 67
    Grilled Tomatillo Salsa, 72
    Jalapeño Salsa, 77
    Crab Guacamole, 44
    Mexican Tenderloin Strips with Avocado, Cheese, and Warm Tortillas, 46

B

Balsamic-Marinated Skirt Steaks with Grilled Smashed Potatoes and Olive Aioli, 78

Barbecue sauces. *See also* Sauces
    Bourbon, 25
    Butcher's Big Red, 107
    Classic Red, 132
    Weber's Tangy, 132
    Whiskey, 18
    Zesty Red, 40
Basics of grilling, 6–13
Basil
    Black Olive Pesto, 51
    Basil-Arugula Pesto, 38
    Basil-Parmesan Butter, 120
Beans
    Black Bean Salsa, 103
    Creamy White Beans, 56
    Roasted Corn and Black Bean Salad, 121
    Smoky Sweet Baked Beans, 125
Big Cowboy Steaks with Whiskey Barbecue Sauce, 18
Black beans
    Black Bean Salsa, 103
    Roasted Corn and Black Bean Salad, 121
Black Olive Pesto, 51
Blue Cheese Vinaigrette, 34
Bone-In Rib-Eye Steaks with Sweet, Pan-Roasted Garlic, 16
Broccolini, 100
Burritos
    Flatiron Steak Burritos with Black Bean Salsa, 103
Butters. *See also* Sauces
    Basil-Parmesan, 120
    Chipotle, 26
    Garlic, 63, 125
    Herb, 100
    Lemon-Parsley, 50, 133
    Louisiana, 120
Buying guide for steak, 6

C

Cajun Corn with Louisiana Butter, 120
Carrots
    Grilled Carrots, 117
Charcoal grilling
    fundamentals, 10, 11
    safety guidelines, 138, 139
Chicago Strip Steaks with Creamy Mustard Sauce, 36
Chuck Steak Sandwiches with Sweet Chili Sauce, 106
Citrus-Marinated Flatiron Kabobs with Scallions, 102
Coconut
    Curry-Coconut Marinade, 85
    Peanut Sauce, 70
    Tomato-Curry Sauce, 20
Corn
    Cajun Corn with Louisiana Butter, 120
    Corn and Tomato Summer Salad, 121
    Corn on the Cob with Basil-Parmesan Butter, 120
    Grilled Vegetable and Orzo Salad, 122
    Roasted Corn and Black Bean Salad, 121
Corn Bread with Bacon and Chives, 124
Couscous Salad, 123
Crab Guacamole, 44
Crostini
    Filet Mignon Crostini with Balsamic Onion Jam, 52
Cucumbers
    Fresh Cucumber Salad, 71
    Pickled Cucumbers, 123
Cuts of steak, 8–9

D, E

Direct and indirect cooking, 10–11
Doneness, 134–135, 136
Dressings
   Blue Cheese Vinaigrette, 34
   Herbed Vinaigrette, 62
   Sesame-Ginger Dressing, 80
   Sherry-Bacon Vinaigrette, 113
   Spicy Asian Dressing, 114
Eggplant
   Eggplant with Spicy Asian
      Dressing, 114
   Vegetable Medley, 66

F

Fajitas
   Skirt Steak Fajitas with Jalapeño
      Salsa, 77
Filet mignon steak, 8
   Filet Mignon Crostini with Balsamic
      Onion Jam, 52
   Filet Mignon Steaks with Black Olive
      Pesto, 51
   Filet Mignon Steaks with Crab
      Guacamole, 44
   Filet Mignon Steaks with Garlicky
      Shrimp, 48
   Filet Mignon Steaks with Orange,
      Hoisin, and Ginger Sauce, 47
   Mexican Tenderloin Strips with
      Avocado, Cheese, and Warm
      Tortillas, 46
   Pepper-Crusted Filet Mignon Steaks
      with Lemon-Parsley Butter, 50

Flank steak, 9
   Flank Steak Gyros with Fresh
      Cucumber Salad, 71
   Flank Steak Marinated in Teriyaki and
      Bourbon, 75
   Flank Steak Satay with Peanut Sauce,
      70
   Italian Beef Sandwiches with Pickled
      Vegetables, 76
   Marinated Flank Steak with Creole
      Flavors, 74
   Pacific Rim Flank Steak with Vegetable
      Medley, 66
   Steak and Tomato Wraps with Avocado
      Sauce, 67
   Steak Tacos with Grilled Tomatillo
      Salsa, 72
   Tagliata of Flank Steak with Arugula
      and Shaved Parmesan, 68
Flatiron steak, 9
   Citrus-Marinated Flatiron Kabobs
      with Scallions, 102
   Flatiron Steak Burritos with Black
      Bean Salsa, 103
   Flatiron Steaks with Herb Butter and
      Grilled Broccolini, 100
   Miso-Marinated Flatiron Steaks with
      Shiitake Mushrooms, 104

G

Garlic
   Garlic Butter, 63, 125
   Grilled Garlic Bread, 125
   Pan-Roasted Garlic, 16
Gas grilling
   fundamentals, 11
   safety guidelines, 138
Ginger Porterhouse Steaks with
   Roasted Sesame Salt, 60
Glazed Sweet Potatoes, 118

Grades of beef, 6
Gremolata, 42
Grilling
   basics of, 6–13
   charcoal grilling, 10, 138, 139
   direct and indirect heat, 10, 11
   gas grilling, 11, 138
   safety guidelines, 138–139
   tools for, 12–13
Grilling guides
   for steak, 134–135
   for vegetables, 137
Guacamole
   Crab Guacamole, 44

H

Hanger steak, 9
   Hanger Steaks with Butcher's Big Red
      Sauce, 107
   Hanger Steaks with Gruyère-Shallot
      Fondue, 108
Herbed Vinaigrette, 62
Hickory Tri-Tip Steak with Chive Cream
   Sauce, 97
Horseradish
   Creamy Horseradish Sauce, 133
   Horseradish-Lemon Cream Sauce, 54
   Horseradish-Tarragon Sauce, 91
   Wasabi-Garlic Sauce, 92

I, J, K, L

Indirect and direct cooking, 10–11
Italian Beef Sandwiches with Pickled
   Vegetables, 76
Jalapeño Salsa, 77

Index

Kabobs
  Citrus-Marinated Flatiron Kabobs, 102
  Peruvian Sirloin Skewers, 90
  Sirloin and Cherry Tomato Kabobs, 88
  Teriyaki Sirloin Kabobs, 86
  Tri-Tip and Zucchini Skewers, 98
Lemon
  Horseradish-Lemon Cream Sauce, 54
  Lemon-Parsley Butter, 50, 135

M

Marbling, 7
Marinades, 129–131
  Bourbon, 25, 130
  Creole, 74
  Cuban, 131
  Curry-Coconut, 85
  Greek, 131
  Lemongrass, 41
  Magical Mediterranean, 131
  Miso, 104
  North Indian, 130
  Pacific Rim, 66
  Spicy Cayenne, 130
  Sweet Soy, 131
  Tequila-Orange, 131
  Teriyaki, 86, 130
  Teriyaki and Bourbon, 75
Marinated Flank Steak with Creole
  Flavors, 74
Market Steaks with Bourbon Barbecue
  Sauce, 25
Mashed Sweet Potatoes with Grilled
  Onions, 118
Melted Onions, 116

Mesquite-Grilled Strip Steaks with
  Worcestershire Paste, 33
Mexican Tenderloin Strips with Avocado,
  Cheese, and Warm Tortillas, 46
Miso-Marinated Flatiron Steaks with
  Shiitake Mushrooms, 104
Mushrooms
  Miso-Marinated Flatiron Steaks with
    Shiitake Mushrooms, 104
  Rosemary-Garlic Skirt Steaks with
    Shiitake Mushrooms, 81
  Strip Steaks with Mushrooms, Bacon,
    and Blue Cheese, 30
Mustard sauces, 36, 94

N, O

New York Steaks with Toasted Fennel
  Spice Rub, 32
New York strip steak. *See* Strip steak
Olives
  Black Olive Pesto, 51
  Olive Aioli, 78
  Tapenade, 133
Onions
  Balsamic Onion Jam, 52
  Grilled Onions, 22, 118
  Melted Onions, 116

P

Pacific Rim Flank Steak with Vegetable
  Medley, 66
Peperonata, 96
Pepper-Crusted Filet Mignon Steaks with
  Lemon-Parsley Butter, 50
Peppered Tri-Tip with Roasted
  Peperonata, 96
Peruvian Sirloin Skewers with Peppers
  and Onions, 90

Pesto
  Basil-Arugula, 38
  Black Olive, 51
Philly-Style Steak Sandwiches, 22
Pickled Cucumbers, 123
Poblano and Cherry Tomato Salsa, 82
Polenta, 88
Porterhouse steak, 8
  Ginger Porterhouse Steaks with
    Roasted Sesame Salt, 60
  Porterhouse Steaks with Béarnaise
    Sauce, 64
  Porterhouse Steaks with Herbed
    Vinaigrette, 62
  Porterhouse Steaks with Spice Crust
    and Garlic Butter, 63
Potatoes
  Grilled Smashed Potatoes, 78
  Twice-Grilled Potatoes, 119

R

Rancho T-Bones with Red Chile-Honey
  Glaze, 57
Really Thick T-Bones with Creamy
  White Beans, 56
Rib-eye steak, 8
  Big Cowboy Steaks with Whiskey
    Barbecue Sauce, 18
  Bone-In Rib-Eye Steaks with Sweet,
    Pan-Roasted Garlic, 16
  Philly-Style Steak Sandwiches, 22
  Market Steaks with Bourbon Barbecue
    Sauce, 25
  Rib-Eye Steaks with Chipotle
    Butter, 26
  Rib-Eye Steaks with Red Wine
    Sauce, 21
  Rib-Eye Steaks with Tomato-
    Chimichurri Sauce, 28

Rib-eye steak, *continued*
    Rib-Eye Steaks with Tomato-Curry
        Sauce, 20
    Straight-Shootin' Cowboy Steaks with
        Toasted Cumin Rub, 24
Roasted Corn and Black Bean Salad, 121
Rosemary-Garlic Skirt Steaks with
    Shiitake Mushrooms, 81
Rubs, 126–128
    Asian, 127
    Beef, 126
    Cajun, 128
    Caribbean, 128
    Classic Barbecue Spice, 127
    Espresso-Chile, 128
    French Roast Spice, 37
    Mexican, 127
    Pick-Me-Up Pepper, 127
    Santa Fe Spice, 84
    Southwest, 128
    Spice, 63
    Tarragon, 128
    Toasted Cumin, 24
    Toasted Fennel Spice, 32
    Type-A, 127

S

Safety guidelines, 138–139
Salads
    Corn and Tomato Summer Salad, 121
    Couscous Salad, 123
    Fresh Cucumber Salad, 71
    Grilled Vegetable and Orzo Salad, 122
    Roasted Corn and Black Bean
        Salad, 121
    Steak and Spinach Salad with
        Sesame-Ginger Dressing, 80
    Steak House Salad with Blue Cheese
        Vinaigrette, 34

Salsas. *See also* Sauces
    Black Bean, 103
    Criolla, 58
    Grilled Tomatillo, 72
    Jalapeño, 77
    Poblano and Cherry Tomato, 82
    Tomato, 133
Salting steaks, 7
Sandwiches. *See also* Tacos
    Easy Chuck Steak Sandwiches, 106
    Flank Steak Gyros, 71
    Flatiron Steak Burritos, 103
    Italian Beef Sandwiches, 76
    Philly-Style Steak Sandwiches, 22
    Skirt-Steak Fajitas, 77
    Steak and Tomato Wraps, 67
    Tri-Tip Steak Sandwiches, 94
Sauces, 132–133. *See also* Barbecue
    sauces; Butters; Salsas
    Avocado, 67
    Basil-Arugula Pesto, 38
    Béarnaise, 64
    Black Olive Pesto, 51
    Bourbon Barbecue, 25
    Butcher's Big Red, 107
    Chive Cream, 97
    Classic Red Barbecue, 132
    Creamy Horseradish, 133
    Creamy Mustard, 36
    Horseradish-Lemon Cream, 54
    Horseradish-Tarragon, 91
    Olive Aioli, 78
    Orange, Hoisin, and Ginger, 47
    Peanut, 70
    Red Wine, 21
    Siren Steak, 132
    Smoked Paprika Aioli, 98
    Sweet Chili, 106
    Tapenade, 133
    Tomato-Chimichurri, 28
    Tomato-Curry, 20
    Wasabi-Garlic, 92

Sauces, *continued*
    Weber's Tangy Barbecue, 132
    Whiskey Barbecue, 18
    Whole-Grain Mustard, 94
    Zesty Red Barbecue, 40
Sesame-Ginger Dressing, 80
Sesame Salt, 60
Sherry-Bacon Vinaigrette, 113
Shrimp
    Garlicky Shrimp, 48
Skewers. *See also* Kabobs
    Flank Steak Satay with Peanut
        Sauce, 70
Skillet Corn Bread with Bacon and
    Chives, 124
Skirt steak, 9
    Balsamic-Marinated Skirt Steaks with
        Grilled Smashed Potatoes and Olive
        Aioli, 78
    Rosemary-Garlic Skirt Steaks with
        Shiitake Mushrooms, 81
    Skirt Steak Fajitas with Jalapeño
        Salsa, 77
    Skirt Steaks with Poblano and Cherry
        Tomato Salsa, 82
    Steak and Spinach Salad with
        Sesame-Ginger Dressing, 80
Smoked Paprika Aioli, 98
Smoky Sweet Baked Beans, 125
Spanish Sirloin Steak with Horseradish-
    Tarragon Sauce, 91
Spicy Asian Dressing, 114
Spinach
    Steak and Spinach Salad with
        Sesame-Ginger Dressing, 80
Squash
    Acorn Squash with Brown Butter and
        Garlic, 114
Steak. *See also* Specific steaks
    buying guide for, 6
    cuts of, 8–9
    doneness, checking for, 135

Index

Steak, *continued*
  grilling guide for, 134–135
  preparation tips, 7
  salting, 7
Steak and Eggs with Gremolata, 42
Steak and Spinach Salad with
  Sesame-Ginger Dressing, 80
Steak and Tomato Wraps with Avocado
  Sauce, 67
Steak House Salad with Blue Cheese
  Vinaigrette, 34
Steak Tacos with Grilled Tomatillo
  Salsa, 72
Straight-Shootin' Cowboy Steaks with
  Toasted Cumin Rub, 24
Strip steak, 8
  Ambassador Steaks with French Roast
    Spice Rub, 37
  Chicago Strip Steaks with Creamy
    Mustard Sauce, 36
  Mesquite-Grilled Strip Steaks with
    Worcestershire Paste, 33
  New York Steaks with Toasted Fennel
    Spice Rub, 32
  New York Strip Steaks with
    Basil-Arugula Pesto, 38
  New York Strip Steaks with Zesty Red
    Barbecue Sauce, 40
  Steak and Eggs with Gremolata, 42
  Steak House Salad with Blue Cheese
    Vinaigrette, 34
  Strip Steaks with Mushrooms, Bacon,
    and Blue Cheese, 30
  Thai Rice Bowl with Lemongrass-
    Marinated Steak, 41
Sweet potatoes
  Glazed Sweet Potatoes, 118
  Mashed Sweet Potatoes, 118

T

Tacos. *See also* Sandwiches
  Mexican Tenderloin Strips with
    Avocado, Cheese, and Warm
    Tortillas, 46
  Steak Tacos with Grilled Tomatillo
    Salsa, 72
Tagliata of Flank Steak with Arugula and
  Shaved Parmesan, 68
Tapenade, 133
T-bone steak, 8
  Argentinean-Style T-Bone Steaks with
    Salsa Criolla, 58
  Rancho T-Bones with Red Chile-
    Honey Glaze, 57
  Really Thick T-Bones with Creamy
    White Beans, 56
  T-Bone Steaks with Horseradish-
    Lemon Cream Sauce, 54
Teriyaki Sirloin Kabobs with Bell Peppers
  and Pineapple, 86
Thai Rice Bowl with Lemongrass-
  Marinated Steak, 41
Tomatoes
  Corn and Tomato Summer Salad, 121
  Poblano and Cherry Tomato Salsa, 82
  Sirloin and Cherry Tomato Kabobs, 88
  Tomato Salsa, 133
Tools for grilling, 12–13
Top sirloin steak, 9
  Peruvian Sirloin Skewers with Peppers
    and Onions, 90
  Sirloin and Cherry Tomato Kabobs
    with Creamy Polenta, 88
  Sirloin Steak Marinated in Curry and
    Coconut, 85
  Sirloin Steaks with Wasabi-Garlic
    Sauce, 92
  Spanish Sirloin Steak with
    Horseradish-Tarragon Sauce, 91

Top sirloin steak, *continued*
  Teriyaki Sirloin Kabobs with Bell
    Peppers and Pineapple, 86
  Top Sirloin Steak with Santa Fe Spice
    Rub, 84
Tri-tip roast (tri-tip steak), 9
  Hickory Tri-Tip Steak with Chive
    Cream Sauce, 97
  Peppered Tri-Tip with Roasted
    Peperonata, 96
  Tri-Tip and Zucchini Skewers with
    Smoked Paprika Aioli, 98
  Tri-Tip Steak Sandwiches with
    Whole-Grain Mustard Sauce, 94
Twice-Grilled Potatoes, 119

U, V, W, Z

USDA grades of beef, 6
Vegetables. *See also* Specific vegetables
  Grilled Vegetable and Orzo Salad, 122
  grilling guide for, 137
  Vegetable Medley, 66
Vinaigrettes. *See* Dressings
White Beans, 56
Zucchini
  Grilled Vegetable and Orzo Salad, 122
  Tri-Tip and Zucchini Skewers with
    Smoked Paprika Aioli, 98
  Vegetable Medley, 66